# GOSSIP

## The Inside Scoop

# GOSSIP
## The Inside Scoop

Jack Levin
and
Arnold Arluke

87-1095

PLENUM PRESS
NEW YORK AND LONDON

Library of Congress Cataloging in Publication Data

Levin, Jack, 1941–
    Gossip: the inside scoop.

    Includes bibliographical references and index.
    1. Gossip. 2. Gossip in mass media. I. Arluke, Arnold, 1947–        . II. Title.
HM263.L473    1987                    302.2'24                    87-2442
ISBN 0-306-42533-5

# ACKNOWLEDGMENTS

We wish to thank those journalists around the country who shared their insights and knowledge. There are some to whom we owe a special debt: James Brady, Iain Calder, Janet Charlton, Marsha Dubrow, Richard Dujardin, Norma Nathan, Sam Rubin, Richard Taylor, and Hal Wingo.

We are also grateful to our colleagues and associates who encouraged our efforts and stimulated our thinking: Allan Kimmel of Fitchburg State College, Fredrick Koenig of Tulane University, William Levin of Bridgewater State College, Earl Rubington of Northeastern University, and Charles Wright of the University of Pennsylvania. The pioneering work of Ralph Rosnow at Temple University inspired our curiosity about the nature of gossip and rumor.

Earle Barcus at Boston University deserves much of the credit for developing our appreciation of content analysis as a tool for understanding mass communication messages.

We benefited a good deal from the presence of competent and conscientious research assistants at Northeastern University who collected and analyzed data which appear throughout the book: Robin Ansher, Kim Becker, Rosemary DeFelice, Jim Howland, Mitchell Jacobs, Michael Lyons, Amita Mody-Desbareau, Lesli Overstreet, Marilla Ross, Joyce Ruscitti, Michele Savran, Jack Schmaly, Karl Seman, Richard Weiner, and Perry Wong.

It was our good fortune to have an editor of the caliber of Linda Greenspan Regan. She applied just the right combination of pressure and patience and provoked major improvements in both the content and the organization of the book.

Finally, we wish to express our gratitude to our families—Flea, Michael, Bonnie, and Andrea Levin and Alyce, Nat, Alan, and Ingrid Arluke. They have always been generous with their encouragement and support and, perhaps more important, with their tolerance and love.

# CONTENTS

# Chapter 1     THE INSIDE SCOOP

Gossip has a bad reputation around town—if not the world. Among the West African Ashanti, nasty or scandalous gossip about a tribal leader is punished by cutting off the gossiper's lips. Only during special ceremonies are members of the tribe allowed to tattle without having their mouths altered. The Seminole Indians of North America treat "talking bad about someone" as they would stealing and lying. They are absolutely convinced that gossiping Indians will lose their place in "Big Ghost City" after they die.[1]

Our culture isn't so different. Americans from diverse backgrounds all share a common disdain for gossip. Some clergy have attacked it on moral grounds. A

3

widely distributed religious pamphlet recently warned churchgoers that "because the tongue is like a tiny spark that sets a huge forest ablaze, there are many ways in which it can be abused." Making reference to both the Old and New Testaments, the pamphlet condemned gossip as "one of the most destructive elements in human nature" because it allows human beings "to make capital of others' faults."[2]

The *New Yorker* also gave a stinging attack on gossip, suggesting that its acceptance marked the disappearance of a quality in the American character that was once pervasive: an absolute intolerance for "the mean, the petty, the unfair, the cheap, the tawdry, the dishonest, and the dishonorable in human nature."[3]

Advice columnist Ann Landers has similarly condemned gossip "as the faceless demon that breaks hearts and ruins careers." In response to one of her troubled letter-writers, whose health and family were being ruined by falsehoods, Ann offered a poem whose more memorable lines included: "My name is Gossip. I maim without killing" and "My victims are helpless. They cannot protect themselves against me because I have no name and no face."[4]

Scholars too have been critical of gossip. Sissela Bok of Brandeis University has drawn on philosophy and psychology to attack gossip in a more serious, academic manner. Whether the gossip is trivial or intentionally malicious, she contends, it is simply wrong because it spreads information that one has promised to keep secret, that one knows to be a lie, or that is unduly invasive. And if one is uncertain about any of these categories of "reprehensible gossip," it is best to remain silent. Trivializing gossip is also wrong, Bok argues, because it brings everyone and everything "down to the lowest common denominator."[5]

Gossip hasn't always had such a bad public image. Originally, the word *gossip* came from the Old English *godsibb*, or "Godparent," a long way from its modern meaning. Prior to the nineteenth century, it was used to refer to men's drinking companions and to the warmth and fellowship between men, not to their talk. During this period, the same term was also used to refer to the friends of a family, usually women, who congregated in the home to await the birth of a child. Gossip was not connected with conversation, although neighbors, friends, and godparents living in small communities would often talk among themselves, especially during the long winter evenings or after the birth of a child. But talk was neither cheap nor dirty; indeed, it was an expression of companionship and community support, if not a primary form of entertainment. In the same way that *God's spell* later became the word *gospel*, the term *godsibb* was transformed into *gossip*.[6]

In 1730, Benjamin Franklin wrote a gossip column in the *Philadelphia Gazette*—and was proud of it. By the beginning of the nineteenth century, however, all of this began to change, and the term *gossip* referred specifically to "idle talk" and "tattling" rather than to a kind of person. According to the Oxford English Dictionary, *gossip* took on the meaning "trifling or groundless rumour; tittle-tattle."[7]

Less than one hundred years later, by the turn of the twentieth century, *gossip* had lost whatever credibility it once possessed. It became essentially what it is now: a code word for sin, sex, and slander; useless small talk; or "catty" backstabbing insults. In everyday conversation, *gossip* no longer referred to a warm, loving relationship; instead, it concerned what happened when the neighborhood "hens" got together to "cluck" about Mrs. Smith's affair with the milkman, Mr. Doe's undiscovered habit of shoplifting from local pharmacies, Miss Jones's alcoholic stupors, the babysitter's uninhibited sexual urges, or Fred's concealed attempt to kill himself.

At the same time that it became synonymous with nastiness, gossip was also more and more regarded as a female activity. It was said that men didn't "gossip"; instead, they engaged in "shop talk" or "locker-room chatter"—they were "shooting the breeze" or "chewing the fat." And those few men unfortunate enough to be caught in the act of "spreading the dirt" were said to be acting like women; they were gossiping "like a bunch of old hens"![8]

Why were women depicted in such a disparaging way as the gossipmongers of society? The mystery of women sharing secrets with other women left much to the male imagination; and the possibility for alliance and solidarity behind the backs of men virtually boggled the masculine mind. Specifically, men feared that at least a certain amount of female companionship involved talk about their husbands' shortcomings and problems. Thus, gossiping threatened men's traditional advantage over women by allowing women to express their discontent collectively— to acknowledge a shared antipathy toward men or at least toward the female's dependent position in life. Even though women were expected to gossip, there was also the suspicion among men that gossip was potentially subversive. Women who did it too much might decide not to stay in their place—in the kitchen and bedroom.

Nineteenth-century authors mirrored men's growing fear of the female gossip by reducing talk among women to nothing more than meaningless, untrue, hostile dribble. *The Gossip's Manual*, published in 1825, satirically belittled the conversations of women by advising them to practice continually their gossiping even if they must talk to themselves. They were encouraged to learn to appear interested in "what ordinary thinkers deem the most trivial things in nature. For example, if Mrs. such-a-one's cat had killed her canary bird, it will furnish a Gossip thus naturally gifted with as much chit chat, as if Mr. such-a-one's wife had lost her favorite child by some horrible death."[9]

If advice books were too subtle, then the sanctions would have to be more direct. By the twentieth century, men routinely prohibited talk among women. In one Texas city of five thousand Chicanos, women were discouraged from meeting—and therefore talking—with any other women outside of their families. During a two-year period, only two cases of regular contact between female neighbors occurred. Both of these women lived alone. In one case, the woman was a widow with no friends or family. Both were severely punished for their disapproved contact.[10]

Despite its bad reputation, we shall argue throughout this book that gossip is often much more than just nasty conversation. Gossip is talk about the public or private lives of other people—both negative and positive, bad and good—especially when those other people aren't around to hear it. As such, gossip gives us the "inside scoop" about others—about their romances, work habits, illnesses, and personal problems; about their children, spouses, and lovers; about their failings and accomplishments, their aspirations and resignations, their indiscretions and idiosyncracies; about anything and everything that is both interesting enough to repeat and obscure enough to be repeatable. Thus, gossip is evaluative. It may describe, but always in order to make a judgment of praise or of blame.

Having the inside scoop is an essential element of gossip and gossiping. *Inside* means that only certain people—the insiders—have been granted the privilege of hearing and passing on a "juicy morsel" or a "shocking revelation." The information being transmitted is typically not yet widely known. Thus, we learn something that others don't know. *Scoop* similarly emphasizes that we got the information first; that we are, at least for the moment, among the privileged few who have it.

Like other aspects of everyday life that we routinely encounter, gossip is rarely chosen as a subject for serious study or research. Rightly or wrongly, we tend to view gossip as trivial by definition—as idle chatter, table talk, or scuttlebutt, as a waste of time for those who do it and therefore as a waste of time for those who might investigate it.

But gossip's reputation leaves numerous questions unanswered. Why would anyone want to know that Clark Gable had bad breath or that he wore dentures?[11] That Lenny Bruce's favorite comic-strip character was the Lone Ranger?[12] That Frank Sinatra once gave Marilyn Monroe a white poodle, which she immediately named "Maf" (short for Mafia)?[13] That presidential assassin Lee Harvey Oswald's favorite television show was the spy series "I Led Three Lives"?[14] That industrial tycoon J. Paul Getty kept a pair of lions at his Sutton Place mansion?[15] That, when she was a child, Margaret Trudeau's parents wouldn't allow her to watch any other television program than "The Ed Sullivan Show"?[16] That Bing Crosby and Rosemary Clooney couldn't read music?[17] That tyrannical dictator Idi Amin was trained as a cook when he first joined the Ugandan army?[18]

In the pages that follow, we explore the who, what, where, and why of gossip. What kind of person is likely to spread gossip? Do women really gossip more than men? How much flattering gossip do people circulate about one another? What do gossip columnists and tabloid reporters have to say about our national celebrities—and about ordinary people? And how do they get the inside scoop when the "stars" refuse to talk to them? How does gossip differ from front-page news? These are among the many questions to which we will address this book.

Rather than rely for our conclusions on stereotypes, unfounded allegations, or popular myth, we take a first-hand look at gossip as it occurs in everyday life, in newspaper columns, in supermarket tabloids—and in places you might least expect to find it. We set aside our preconceptions and our prejudices to develop a portrait of gossip, the gossipmonger, and the target of gossip.[19]

Obviously, to do this, our book must provide numerous examples of gossip. Although we make no claims about the accuracy of this gossip, it is all "real," that is, part of our culture and its folklore about the famous. What follows, then, is certainly more than a book of gossip; it is the inside scoop on a much maligned, much neglected, yet often important, aspect of everyday life.

# Chapter 2    THE PSYCHOLOGY OF GOSSIP

To regard gossip as "idle chatter" is to underestimate its usefulness. Why do people gossip? In the larger scheme of things, why has gossip survived throughout the centuries in every known society under the most hostile conditions, regardless of the local laws and customs designed to obliterate it?

At the extreme, the need for gossip is so acutely felt that some small societies actually hold annual ceremonies for the express purpose of permitting the group members to say anything they want to about one another. At the other end of the continuum, the people in certain societies share an exaggerated sense of privacy and prohibit gossiping through the strictest local rules or laws.[1]

In some Mexican villages, for example, villagers are intensely apprehensive about being the target of gossip and about being charged with spreading gossip about others. Despite their personal concerns, however, these villagers still have an insatiable curiosity about the private affairs of their neighbors and kin. They are fascinated with disclosures and slips in other people's lives. In fact, when adequate gossip is not available, it is commonplace for spying between households to occur. Any unusual or ambiguous episode down the road or in a neighbor's yard is excuse enough to send a child from the family to get a firsthand view, which he or she is expected to report back to the parents.[2]

We believe that gossip survives and prospers universally precisely because it is psychologically useful. Where gossip occurs, we can usually identify one or more gossipers who bring the message to a group and one or more listeners who receive the message. Gossip is frequently useful for both gossipers and listeners. Less obviously, it may also serve functions for the targets of gossip, whose activities and characteristics are being discussed in their absence.

What does gossip do for the gossiper? Some people are "other-directed"; they have a powerful need to be accepted by their peers, to do the things in life that will gain them esteem in the eyes of their friends and associates, and to have the "inside scoop." By making some people insiders, gossip may serve the social needs of other-directed people. But just how far will they go to impress their friends?

To find out, we decided to spread some gossip among the college students on our campus (young people are notorious for their other-directedness). So we printed hundreds of flyers announcing a wedding ceremony in front of the student union on our campus. They read, "You are cordially invited to attend the wedding of Robert Goldberg and Mary Ann O'Brien on June 6 at 3:30 in the afternoon." We saturated our campus with the flyers, tacking them to every bulletin board and door in sight, leaving them on desks in the classrooms of every building.

Of course, the two "students," Robert Goldberg and Mary Ann O'Brien, were as ficticious as the event itself. The flyers announced the date of the wedding as June 6. But we didn't distribute the flyers until June 7, so that students on campus thought they had missed the wedding by one day. Then, we waited. In fact, we waited seven days in order to give our gossip about the wedding a chance to spread throughout the campus. And spread it did. One week after distributing the flyers, we questioned a sample of students to determine how many had heard about the wedding. Incredibly, more than half—52 percent—knew about it, usually through their friends and classmates who had seen the flyers tacked up around the campus. More amazingly, 12 percent told us they had actually attended the wedding! These students said they were there on June 6; many of them described the "white wedding gown" worn by the bride and the "black limo" that drove the newlyweds to their honeymoon destination.

At first, we thought there might actually have been a wedding on campus that had coincidentally taken place at about the same time and place as the one we had fabricated. But after careful checking, we ruled out that possibility and concluded instead that 12 percent of the students we questioned had lied about having been at the wedding.

Is this so unusual? Certain events are so "special" that many otherwise decent, ordinary people may falsely claim to have attended or, at the very least, to have contemplated attending, even if they haven't. They don't want to feel "left out," so they weave tales—sometimes tall tales—concerning people at parties, get-togethers, baseball games, dances, bars, or tennis matches—people they have actually never seen and know nothing about. People who may not even exist, except in the wish fulfillment of gossipmongers.

The implication of our "experiment" is clear: gossip is often used to place people at the center of attention. If you have the inside scoop about the BIG EVENT, you will be regarded as an insider. Even better, you actually attended the BIG EVENT. That makes you special.

But are gossipmongers usually the gregarious, sociable types who already have lots of friends with whom they can gossip? In a study of the alleged death of Paul McCartney in 1969, two social psychologists found that those individuals who initially helped spread this false gossip were actually less popular, dated less often, and had fewer contacts with friends than individuals who "dead-ended" the story.[3]

Because gossip often places people at the center of attention, it also, at least temporarily, enhances their status with others. This may explain why gossipmongers come from the most isolated, least popular members of a group. After all, they are the ones who most need something to make them socially acceptable.

In the long run, however, a person who gossips too much may lose status in the eyes of his or her friends and associates. He or she may become defined as a "bigmouth" or a "yenta" who will "talk to anyone about anything," as a person who cannot be trusted to keep a secret or to be discreet with "privileged information." In addition, some manipulative individuals, knowing the gossiper's predilection, may purposely feed false information to the gossiper for personal gain or even malice.

Celebrity gossip may similarly have the function of placing an individual at the center of attention and making her or him more attractive and powerful in the eyes of colleagues or friends. According to professional gossip Barbara Howar, the self-aggrandizement function of gossip is important: "When you say, 'I was at Le Cirque yesterday, sitting next to Bill Buckley and Liz Smith, and I heard them talking about Abe Rosenthal [editor of the *New York Times*], and then Buckley said something about Kissinger,' you are also saying, 'I've been out to swell lunches, I know swell people, I've heard swell things, I'm wonderful.' "[4]

It is, of course, second best to pass on gossip secondhand, but, for someone starved for attention, that will have to do. If you can't be there, you can at least read about it in gossip columns, tabloids, or biographies—and then circulate the gossip to your friends and associates. This works especially well when the gossip reveals the unexpected, when it fails to confirm our suspicions and contains an element of surprise.

Take biographical accounts of the infamous celebrity Adolph Hitler.[5] Much of the dirt about him is quite consistent with his demonic and cruel image. At dinner parties, he would delight in making cute conversation about medieval torture techniques. When asked what he would do upon landing in England, Hitler replied without hesitation that he wanted most to see the place where Henry VIII chopped off the heads of his wives. Hitler's personal idea for executing the German generals who had plotted to overthrow him was to hang each man on a meathook and slowly strangle each to death with piano wire, periodically releasing the pressure to intensify the death agonies.

Yet this murderer of millions was, at the same time, very concerned about protecting his animal friends. One of his most heartfelt concerns was for the suffering of lobsters and crabs. He even had his high officials debate the question of the most humane death for lobsters—whether to place them in water brought slowly to a boil or to place them quickly in boiling water. Despite Hitler's legendary sadism, he was a masochist about sex. It is reported that he ordered young women to squat over him and urinate or defecate on his head. One of his dates claimed that after she and Adolph had undressed, he got down on the floor, condemned himself as unworthy, groveled around in an agonized manner, and begged her to kick him—which she did. What really pops the Hitlerian mystique is that his favorite movie was supposedly *Snow White and the Seven Dwarfs* and that his favorite actress was Shirley Temple.

Although gossip may put people at the center of attention, must it always be done at someone's expense? With this question in mind, we examined 194 instances of gossip as they occurred in the conversations of 76 male and 120 female college students at a large university.[6] Actually, we didn't collect the evidence ourselves; that would have been too conspicuous (professors don't sit in the student lounge, except in rare circumstances). Instead, we had two students act as trained observers. For eight weeks, they sat much of the school day in the student lounge, a central area of the university in which large numbers of undergraduates congregate to talk, study, and read. And for eight weeks, they eavesdropped on their fellow students' conversations.

The study had some surprising results: According to our observers, whereas 27 percent of all student gossip was clearly positive, 27 percent was clearly negative—only 27 percent! (The rest was mixed.) This is probably far less negative gossip than most people might have predicted, as gossip is so often associated with nasty talk only.

Thinking that more pernicious gossip might emerge under the influence of alcohol, we then repeated the same study in an area of the campus center where beer and wine were served. The results obtained in this "bar" setting were almost identical to those we got in the student lounge. Is it possible that people tend to say just as many nice as nasty things about other people? Perhaps we are mistaken to reserve the label *gossip* for nasty talk only. Moreover, we may tend to remember only the nasty things that people say about one another.

Much of the students' gossip, we discovered—both positive and negative—concerned personal habits, manners, appearance, and role performance. On the negative side, students typically complained about such public displays of "gross" personal habits as "nail biting," "eating with your mouth open," and "belching in public"; about teachers who "are clumsy and drop things all the time" and "fail to comment on papers"; about the ostentatious behavior of a "Jewish-American Princess"; about rudeness on a commuter train; and about an "ugly girl" who walks awkwardly. Among the nice things said of others, a student praised a football player who "played a good game," another complimented a classmate who "always looks nice," and still another spoke well of a relative who helped one of the students to bed "after a bad drunk" and discussed the virtues of "a real nice looker."

Our results also bear directly on whether women are gossipmongers. First of all, the women being observed devoted more of their conversations to discussions of other people (rather than the weather, sports, homework, and so on) than did the men being observed. If this is gossip, then these college women did indeed gossip more than their male counterparts on campus. If, however, gossip is regarded as only nasty or derogatory talk about others, then a different picture emerges.

Before we discuss what that picture looks like, let us emphasize again that many people associate gossip only with derogatory, even scandalous, information about the lives of others. It is frequently in this context that the woman has been portrayed as a gossip. Our results indicated instead that both male and female gossip contained the same amount of clearly positive and clearly negative references to others. In this sense of the term, women were no more likely than men to gossip, at least not at the college campus we studied.

Despite similarities in the tone of their conversations, college men and women differed markedly in their targets of gossip. Women were much more likely than men to talk about close friends and family members, whereas men were likely to talk about celebrities, including sports figures, as well as about other acquaintances on campus (for example, their classmates in a large lecture course).

Sex differences may reflect what we have traditionally expected men and women to do with their lives and the opportunities we have given them to interact with different kinds of people. Until the women's movement, feminine activities were confined to family and friendship networks, whereas masculine activities involved instrumental, more distant relationships. Even today, preteen and teenaged boys and girls differ in the kinds of people they associate with: boys are likely to have extensive peer relations, and girls are likely to have intensive peer relations. Reflecting their opportunities for interacting with others, when boys talk they tend to stress goal- and action-oriented activities; when girls talk, they are more likely to discuss topics of an intensely personal and private nature. In their gossip, then, women focus more on their close relationships, with mothers, sisters, best friends, and the like. Men, in contrast, maintain their psychological distance by discussing strangers, acquaintances, and media celebrities—disk jockeys, coaches, TV personalities, and members of large classes on campus. In terms of sex roles, the male students may have been "afraid to get close." Even in their gossip, they were unable or unwilling to express intimate feelings or intense emotion concerning the most important people in their lives. Traditionally, this attitude has been associated with the male role.

Gossipmongers also benefit from gossip in a more insidious sense. It permits the gossiper to communicate negative, even nasty, information about other people with impunity, regardless of its consequences for the well-being of the targets. People are allowed to gossip about things they might never acknowledge in a public setting. They become the bearers of bad tidings.

Some people prefer to keep quiet rather than to repeat unpleasant news. Their reticence is understandable: others might see them as enjoying the suffering of the victim or even of having caused it. Psychologists call this phenomenon the *mum effect*; they indicate that it applies specifically to the situation of informing someone else about his or her misfortune and not to bad news in general. For example, one might be reluctant to tell Herman that his wife has been sleeping around, but one might not hesitate to give Herman's friends the same information. Therefore, gossip becomes a vehicle for the transmission of bad news—news that probably would not be communicated directly to the victim.

Under such conditions, gossip can become negative, even vicious, being a convenient method for attacking those we despise or seek revenge against. Gossip allows individuals to say otherwise private things without taking responsibility. After all, they are "only passing on what others have said. Don't blame me. I didn't start it." This attitude may have therapeutic benefits, as in most psychotherapy, for someone who might otherwise not be able to "get it out of his or her system" or "let off steam," but it also gives gossip its bad reputation. Just as gossip relieves tension, it also tends to relieve nagging guilt.

For the listeners, gossip is informal news about other people.[7] In nonliterate societies, gossip is a method of storing and retrieving information about the social environment.[8] Among the Hopi Indians, for example, current trials and conflicts between individuals are influenced by gossip about previous disputes and legal precedents.[9]

In order to survive in modern society, we, too, must understand more than just the physical environment. We must also understand the social environment—those people with whom we work and play. In a mass society, we typically work in a division of labor in which we are forced to rely on others. Government, corporations, and big business all require knowledge of others. Indeed, in entire careers—for example, social work, psychology, marketing, and public relations—the central component is human relations. For anyone to be successful in such a career, a facility with gossip is absolutely essential.

Gossip can give us advice about how best to lead our lives. When we hear that Humphrey Bogart was blunt about discussing the cancer that killed him, we are also being instructed about the right way to die—being open rather than ashamed about having a disease like cancer. We might also be advised to strip away the complexities of our lives. Those who knew Albert Einstein noted that his secret to personal happiness was simplicity in all phases of his life, right down to the clothes he wore.

Gossip can also help explain why people behave as they do: why they are so unhappy, why they have had five divorces, or why they can't hold down a job. Although not necessarily accurate, such gossip arises because some behavior or event is important enough to demand an explanation. This is especially true when we deal with matters of life and death.

For example, the death of actress Natalie Wood generated a lot of gossip to account for the tragedy. Some sources said that drinking caused her to slip and fall into the water while she was on a boat with her husband Robert Wagner. Others whispered that she had an incurable disease which altered her balance and caused her to take the final plunge.

Gossip can be a medium for sharing the culture of one's workplace either through the office grapevine or even through formal office meetings. In a study of high-tech organizations in California's Silicon Valley, employee gossip was found to identify heroes and villains, and to reflect attitudes and values of the company. The gossip of workers at places like IBM, Hewlett-Packard, and Digital Equipment often focused on equality, security, and control. Gossip also helped newly hired employees to "learn the ropes" by providing information about what to expect from the boss (for example, "Will he come on to female employees?" or "Will he chew you out if you make a mistake?"). The newcomer also learned which co-workers should be avoided because their personalities were obnoxious or because they never paid back loans. Conversely, newcomers heard who was good to talk with when they had personal problems or who would stick up for them when work fell behind schedule.[10]

Employees also exchanged stories about people that communicated, correctly or incorrectly, the likelihood of being promoted or fired, for example, "Joe has been here for six years, does great work, has been promised a better job and look where he is now—right where he started!" Gossip on the job, then, reflects basic survival issues faced by employees. This kind of informal "on-the-job training" is every bit as essential as the formal training in classrooms and apprenticeships.

Whether on or off the job, gossipers must be at least familiar enough with one another to reduce social distance to a minimum. This may require being of the same age, gender, race, religion, or social class. Most important, in order to gossip together, people must share the same set of values and must know a third person in common whose behavior either upholds or violates those values.

Furthermore, gossip is used to maintain the dividing line between those who are part of the "in group" and those who are not. To gossip is to indicate that the teller and the recipient share a degree of closeness or intimacy not necessarily shared with others. Thus, gossip can be a sign of trust between people which can create and maintain boundaries around "in-group" members.[11] It demonstrates "relative intimacy and distance and can become a device for manipulating relationships, for forging new intimate ones and discarding old, less attractive ones."[12] For example, someone who moves into a new neighborhood where he is initially a stranger to all will feel accepted when he gets the neighborhood "dirt." At that point, he has been given the stamp of approval by those who control informal information in the community. He has now "made it" as a member-in-good-standing of the neighborhood. In a similar way, people at a cocktail party may group themselves by confiding in some but not in others. Outsiders feel "left out," and insiders are made to feel comfortable.

This function of gossip ensures that certain stories will be told and retold over a long period of time, whenever the cohesiveness of a group needs reinforcement. Even decades after graduating, individuals who come together for a class reunion will often replay the same old stories about what John did in his senior year of high school, what Mary used to do at the back of her algebra class, how Al cheated his way through English, and the like. For similar reasons, a new employee may know that she is accepted by fellow workers when they allow her to hear the 488th telling of the story about what the boss did at the Christmas party ten years ago.[13] Gossip also underscores the differences between insiders and outsiders on the job.

In a sense, gossip is the glue that binds individuals together, especially in societies marked by rampant loneliness. Indeed, under such conditions, gossip may be the only available means of reducing isolation in modern society. It may represent the closest that many of us will ever come to experiencing genuine intimacy and integration.

One psychiatrist claims, for instance, that the telephone party line has saved more people from nervous breakdowns than any other remedy.[14] They no longer feel alone if they spread as well as listen to the gossip of others. A good gabfest is, by its very nature, interpersonal, even if it is only talk over telephone lines. The person who never gossips simply may not be interested in human behavior; on the other hand, he or she may have no friends to gossip about. Talk with and about others may provide as much psychological gratification as actual interaction; they both may meet a need for the warmth of human relationships. Not surprisingly, surveys show that well-adjusted people are more interested in human behavior than in anything else.

Even among those who engage in everyday gossip, sociologists report that loneliness is a major problem of modern life. Many city dwellers are detached from traditional neighborhood life. In our mass society, many people move thousands of miles from family and friends for schooling, another job, or love. How can they ever hope to make up for the loss in human relationships?

With the help of celebrity gossip, famous people become familiar friends. We often get to know more about the details of their personal lives than we know about the real people around us. The television camera follows them as they break up with their lovers, overdose on drugs, mourn the deaths of close friends, and eat breakfast. They become so much a part of our lives that we treat them as one of the family. When actor Robert Young played the role of Doctor Marcus Welby, he received 200,000 letters asking for medical advice. Hundreds of angry women picketed the studios of NBC-TV to protest the "killing" of soap opera character Marlena Evans. Even the birth of a soap opera baby is a personal event: thousands of viewers typically send cards and gifts to celebrate the joyous event. Welcome to the neighborhood!

For listeners, gossip is also an important source of entertainment and relaxation. Some of what we regard as gossip is indeed "intellectual chewing gum"—trivial or insignificant, originating in a shared desire for "new experience." Its triviality doesn't necessarily preclude its being interesting.[15]

Informal gatherings convened for the purpose of playing cards, welcoming newcomers to the neighborhood, taking a break on the job, or eating dinner with friends often provide an excuse to gossip. In reality, the manifest purpose for meeting takes a backseat to conversation. Individuals become so engrossed in gossip that they may decide to modify their original plans for the evening so as to accommodate their need for gossip; a card game is transformed into a lively talk over drinks; several employees take their coffee breaks together to swap information about their new boss; over the dinner table, the members of a family discuss the sexual activities of a neighbor.

The appeal of everyday gossip is also responsible for mass media forms of entertainment in which gossip plays a part. Ten million people weekly read such gossip tabloids as *The National Enquirer*, *The Star*, *The National Examiner*, and *The Globe*. Millions more read *People* and *Us* on a regular basis. Dozens of gossip columnists appear in local newspapers across the country, many in syndicated versions. Talk shows on radio and television invite callers to phone in questions and comments, frequently concerning sexual behavior, politicians, or Hollywood celebrities. The long-standing popularity of "The Tonight Show" with Johnny Carson is in part based on the talent of its host for asking the same questions of celebrity guests that the ordinary viewer would ask: "Is it true that you are dating another man?" "How did your marriage end?" "How did you feel about playing opposite your ex-lover?" This format provides an opportunity for viewers to confirm the gossip that they have read in gossip columns and magazines.

Escape is an important part of the entertainment appeal of celebrity gossip. It permits the members of an audience to retreat into the glamorous, extravagant lifestyles of the rich and famous. Hearing the details of another person's exotic or extraordinary lifestyle helps us psychologically to avoid, if only momentarily, the difficult aspects of our own lives. For example, gossip about Aristotle Onassis and Jackie Kennedy's incessant spending sprees may have allowed us to play out our wildest fantasies.[16] Insiders claim that in Onassis and Jackie's first year of marriage, the couple's personal expenditures ran at the incredible rate of $20 million. They had a villa in Monte Carlo with seven servants, a penthouse in Paris with five servants; a hacienda in Montevideo, Uruguay, with thirty-eight servants; a villa in Glyfada, Greece, with ten servants; a Fifth Avenue apartment in New York City with five servants; a private island in the Ionian Sea with seventy-two servants; and a yacht with a crew of sixty-five. The annual salary for their chefs alone totaled almost $750,000. Security for both of them came to a mere $84,000 yearly.

For an American version of escape gossip, recall the extravagent expenditures of billionaire Howard Hughes.[17] The mysterious recluse had enough money to buy thirteen private planes (in addition to his controlling interest in TWA) and seven resort casinos in Las Vegas. Reporters and aides to Hughes revealed that he also purchased KLAS-TV in Las Vegas because he liked to watch the late movies; the station refused to run them all night long, so he became its owner.

Bizarre gossip helps us escape, too. And many of Hughes's habits were off the wall. Did you know that Hughes liked sweets so much that he sometimes went for weeks eating nothing but candy, cookies, and milk? He went for another long stretch eating only Campbell's chicken soup. When it came to ice cream, he ate nothing but Baskin-Robbins banana nut. And he would drink only Poland Spring water in quart containers from the company's original Maine plant. Reclusive Hughes was so phobic about germs that any document delivered to him had to be typed by a secretary wearing white gloves and hand-delivered by a gloved courier. Because of his fear of germs, he also would not walk from his bed to the bathroom without laying a pathway of paper towels to walk on. When Hughes discovered Arby's sandwiches, he decided to try them, but only if the local Arby's shop obtained a special stainless steel blade to be used only for slicing the beef for his sandwiches. At one point, his phobia got so out of hand that all inanimate objects, like silverware, had to be wrapped in Kleenex when handed to him. Even weirder, he insisted that a second layer of Kleenex be used so the original wrapping wouldn't get contaminated.

Of course, there is also happy gossip that makes us feel good about the world. There are times when we may gossip to uplift and enhance people by embellishing their virtues and ignoring their faults. Elvis Presley's fans never stop citing his extraordinary generosity.[18] Many of his family and friends were given cars by Elvis—the first being his mother, who received a pink Cadillac. Elvis liked seeing movies and would rent out a local movie theatre and allow as many as a hundred fans to share the pictures with him. During his psychic period, Elvis thought he could spiritually heal people. Despite his pressured schedule, he made his healing services available to all the people in his circle at any time.

There is always gossip about Frank Sinatra's legendary generosity.[19] According to gossip columnist Earl Wilson, Sinatra once tipped a parking lot attendant $100, made a free singing commercial for a car dealer, and gave everything away to maids and waiters after finishing a movie, including TVs, radios, and liquor. Wilson also claims that Sinatra once gave his friends Rosalind Russell and Frederick Brisson a party for their twenty-fifth wedding anniversary costing $25,000. Sinatra also converted his plane to a hospital jet to fly medical people to Barbados for the purpose of treating Claudette Colbert's sick husband.

Many people, at one time or another, evaluate themselves by comparing their abilities, opinions, or achievements with those of other people. Gossip may be a reasonable and nonpainful way to obtain needed comparison information which coud not have been obtained directly.[20]

One purpose of comparing oneself with others is to provide one with heroes or role models. Much gossip about celebrities has the effect of increasing the identification of audience members with their celebrity heroes. When a columnist describes what Robert Redford eats for breakfast, her message is that Redford isn't so different from us after all. Not only does he eat breakfast, but he eats pretty much the same kind of breakfast that we do. Therefore, Robert Redford is a flesh-and-blood human being with whom we can more easily identify. He can be seen as a competent, attractive actor who also has human qualities.

Through gossip about celebrities, the public is able to visualize the life of a hero and even to enjoy it vicariously. Celebrities are depicted while swimming in their pools and sunning themselves on their yachts, or dining in expensive restaurants and dating other celebrities. Knowing the intimate details of celebrity lifestyles helps the public feel close to its heroes—to reduce the anonymity and impersonality which have become associated with life in a mass society.

Gossip about members of the community whom we hold in high esteem provides levels of aspiration for our own behavior. We know that others have "made it" and that they deserve our praise. On a more personal level, however, we are now convinced that we can make it, too.

People often use this kind of gossip to remind them of the pot of gold at the end of their rainbow—the rewards that they may expect to obtain because of a successful career. Those who believe that their own lives will be marked by great wealth look for models who have already "made it" to indicate how they may spend the millions of dollars they will surely acquire in the future. Those who look foward to having great power seek models in powerful figures whose lifestyles may be worthy of imitation. Success-oriented people want to know about the extravagant lifestyle of billionaire J. Paul Getty.[21] They want to know that he once gave a party for twelve hundred guests who consumed thirty-four bottles of vodka, thirty-nine bottles of gin, fifty-four bottles of brandy, one hundred and seventy-four bottles of whiskey, and several hundred bottles of beer and soft drinks. They also ate one hundred pounds of caviar. Success-oriented people want the details of J. Paul Getty's life. They may be interested to learn that Getty enjoyed reading gossipy newspapers, that the walls of his indoor pool were covered with Italian marble, that he sometimes received as many as two hundred letters a day that begged him to contribute money to some cause, or that he loved eating fudge, maple walnut ice cream, waffles with maple syrup, and Cadbury's milk chocolate. Success-oriented people may also be happy to find out that J. Paul Getty had human frailties as well: he was scared to death of being near anyone with a cold; he was a pill popper who daily took large quantities of medications; and he was extremely superstitious and would refuse to sit thirteen at a table. Regarding the way he spent (or didn't spend) his money, Getty installed a pay telephone in the lobby of his mansion for the use of visitors.

Even negative gossip can serve to enhance the process of identification with a celebrity figure. A little "dirt" makes an unapproachable idol into a flesh-and-blood human being with frailties just like the rest of us. We may even like her or him better as a result.[22]

Much of the negative information about well-known people in gossip columns and tabloids consists of reports about their violations of the small rules of life. When it comes to our national heroes, this is precisely what we want to read or hear: nothing horrible, but just enough dirt to make human beings out of larger-than-life idols; nothing disgraceful, but just enough filth to pull them down a peg or two; nothing monstrous, but just enough nastiness to make it possible for an average Joe Schmo to identify with his big-shot heroes.

Gossip can knock our celebrities down a peg or two from their superhuman status by revealing their bad habits, silly preoccupations, and unflattering characteristics.

A movie star of the stature of Bette Davis becomes a little less a legend when we discover that her big brown eyes were actually quite average in size, and that she would chemically dilate her pupils to make her eyes look larger than life.[23] Or that Rosemary Clooney was in psychotherapy for years. After Robert F. Kennedy's death, she had to be institutionalized. Rosemary's husband, actor Jose Ferrer, cheated on her even before they had packed the bags for their honeymoon.[24] Or when flapper par excellence Joan Crawford got up in the morning, her short red hair would stand straight up, resembling an explosion of firecrackers on the Fourth of July.[25] Or Elvis Presley was so self-conscious of his "chicken neck" that he would wear high collars to disguise it. What bothered him even more was his embarrassingly small penis, which he called "Little Elvis." We all have friends who are plagued with weight problems. The great beauty Elizabeth Taylor is no different. She even lost starring roles in several films because she was so fat.[26]

The most popular celebrity biographies almost always print a little dirt. Marilyn Monroe's former maid and trusted confidante wrote extensively, for example, about the celebrated sex symbol's unfortunate childhood, during which her mother dragged her from one foster home to another until her rape by a "foster father" resulted in a pregnancy.[27] At the age of fifteen, she gave birth to a baby boy, who was immediately taken from her to be adopted. She never saw him again. On her way to the top, Marilyn had a homosexual affair with her first drama teacher. As a young woman, she tried prostitution as an easy way to make extra money. She also enjoyed seeing how excited her customers would become when she took off her clothes. But the most depressing years of Marilyn

Monroe's life may well have been the last six, when she was unhappily married to Arthur Miller and spent most of the day in her small, simple bedroom. Outside of appointments with a psychiatrist and her acting teacher, Marilyn's daily routine consisted of sleeping, looking at herself in the mirror, drinking champagne, and speaking on the phone.

The dirt in Marilyn Monroe's biographies probably does little to tarnish her memory. She is essentially depicted as an insecure, emotionally needy person who never saw herself as attractive and believed that other people were laughing at her. More likely, a detailing of the unsavory elements of her life only serves to make her into a less-than-perfect human being who was a victim of circumstances over which she had little control. The result is to arouse sympathy in those who can identify with her and to explain why a beautiful and successful Hollywood idol would take her own life.

By contrast, gossip about those who are considered "immoral" or "inferior" serves to enhance our own feelings of respectability and self-worth. By comparison with their illegal, illicit, immoral activities, we can feel some satisfaction with ourselves. This relative notion of self-worth and personal morality is a cultural variable, being especially associated with competitive Western societies. In America, for example, feelings of respectability are dependent on downgrading the moral character of others. There is a zero-sum definition of the situation, in which the identification of immorality is essential for the maintenance of self-worth.[28]

Social psychologists have shown what may be the origin of the relative definition of individual morality. They suggest that American children are extremely competent in playing competitive games in which only one winner is possible. For instance, American children feel a personal gain in games in which their peers are deprived of rewards. In other words, another child's loss is regarded as a personal gain.[29]

Sometimes we like gossip that does more than merely knock celebrities down a notch. To some, what is interesting is the monstrous and grotesque side of the lives of public figures. Gossip about their peculiar excesses, their insatiable appetites for drugs, sex, or fame, and their bizarre habits may revolt us, yet such talk also transports us into a nightmarish world about which most of us are curious.

A gossip book about Elvis Presley, for example, tells all.[30] We learn that Elvis brushed his teeth with Colgate; that he wore one-half-inch lifts in his bedroom slippers; and that he couldn't read music. But why did this book become a best-seller, with over 100,000 copies in print? Is it merely because the biographer gossips about Elvis's $10,000 tuxedo or his secret desire to become a Jew? Unlikely. The best explanation for the striking success of the Elvis biography is that it portrays Elvis as a gluttonous and sadistic madman reminiscent of the notorious Roman emperor Caligula. Picture Elvis eating with his hands (while his pinky remains erect in the air) his favorite meal, consisting of one pound of crisp bacon, four orders of mashed potatoes with thick gravy, a large portion of sauerkraut, a dish of crowder peas, and a stack of tomatoes. Then, a few hours later, Elvis has a compulsive munchie attack and he consumes thirty containers of yogurt or $100 worth of popsicles. For fun, Elvis might watch TV until he dislikes a particular show, at which point he would shoot out the TV screen with one of the two .45's slung around his waist. Or he might decide to step outside and fire his M-16 machine gun at one of the small buildings behind his house until it was set ablaze. For an even better time, the King might get his boys together and play "war"—a game Elvis devised where two teams go at each other with several thousand dollars' worth of Roman candles, skyrockets, and firecrackers until someone gets hurt.

For a different sort of fun, Elvis secretly watched other people making love through a special two-way mirror installed in his home, until he became sufficiently aroused to quickly penetrate his own companion. As a token of his appreciation, he awarded his star-struck bed companion a .38 Python. If voyeurism wasn't Elvis's thing that night, then he might invite an entire chorus line of dancers to join him in his hotel suite in Paris or simply pick any three or four of the many female admirers who showed up each night to join him on his 9-foot x 9-foot double-king-sized bed (with retractable armrests), flanked on one side with a large photo of his mother and on the other with a portrait of Jesus Christ.

What is the appeal of gossip that makes celebrities into childlike monsters, indulging every whim and fantasy they have? Psychologists observe that people made instantly rich by winning the "big lottery" almost never achieve the happiness they expect. In fact, they usually are more depressed than ever.[31] For the average guy who will never win the million-dollar lottery, it is comforting to discover that fame and wealth, and the power that follows, are not always tickets to happiness.

The gossip about Liz Taylor's extravagances is a case in point.[32] While Liz had chili dinners flown from Los Angeles to Paris and had hundreds of real diamonds sewn to her dresses to avoid the cheap look of rhinestones, she also went through the miseries of seven divorces and several periods of excessive drinking.

Even more tragic is the story of George Sanders, the Oscar-winning actor. His constant worldwide traveling and his ability to playfully speculate with over a million dollars in business deals did little to make him satisfied with life. At the age of sixty-five he killed himself with a handful of sleeping pills. Sanders left a note which read, "I am committing suicide because I am bored. I feel I have lived long enough. I leave you all in your sweet little cesspool and I wish you luck."[33]

Celebrities aren't the only ones with problems. Tabloids like the *National Enquirer* or the *Star* occasionally print stories about people who are "down and out," lonely, penniless, or sick. Although it may be hard to hear unhappy gossip, it may make our own problems pale by comparison. How can anyone worry about living on a meager income when he finds out that Gerry and Darlene Vanderpool of Downey, California, had so little money that they shared only one can of tomato soup a week and that Darlene tried to sell one of her kidneys to get some extra money for food. Are you having problems with your spouse? A forty-one-year-old Canadian man was so jealous about his wife's cheating that he kept her locked in a small box every night. When he let her sleep with him, he handcuffed her to his body.

Some celebrity gossip is based more on a morbid curiosity about the misfortunes of those more famous than we. Misery loves miserable company—especially when the miserable are rich, famous, and apparently successful: See, life at the top isn't what it's cracked up to be, now is it?

The afternoon soap operas are filled with gossip about successful, wealthy, and beautiful people who are downright miserable.[34] The average middle-class, middle-aged housewife has problems of her own, of course. She's concerned about her husband's flirtatious behavior at the office, about her son's bad grade in algebra, about how she and her husband will make next month's mortgage payment to the bank. But all of her problems, no matter how severe, are eclipsed by the infidelity, murders, suicides, rapes, drug abuse, and incest that have become part and parcel of serials in the afternoon.

To make things even more appealing, the average soap is written in such a way that the audience can snoop on the characters and observe their reactions.[35] Actually, the popularity of daytime serials (and their primetime counterparts, like "Dallas" and "Dynasty") depends a good deal on gossip. Everyday, Monday through Friday (barring a news bulletin or a presidential address), we follow our "good friends" into their offices, living rooms, and bedrooms. We are guests at their weddings and funerals; we visit them in the hospital after surgery or the birth of their children. We "snoop on them" while they argue with their spouses, make love, and punish their children. Indeed, we get to know more about the personal lives of our favorite soap opera characters than we know about our real neighbors who have lived next door for the past seventeen years (whose names we may never have learned). Soap operas consist of talk, talk, and more talk.

The voyeuristic element in gossip can also be seen in soap operas. Typically, the audience is let in on a problem, a resolution, or a crisis long before the characters are. By concealing information from a character, but not the audience, we are able to "snoop" in a way that would otherwise be impossible. We know what they don't. We can therefore evaluate their emotional reactions. We can even place ourselves in their shoes. For example, on "Days of Our Lives," we know that Hope has gone with Patch to Stockholm in order to find a witness whose courtroom testimony could exonerate Bo. Bo has no idea. In fact, he believes that Patch has forced Hope to go along with him. On "General Hospital," Luke doesn't know that Laura has been kidnapped. But we do.

So far we've focused on the people who gossip and on their reasons for doing so. Is it possible that gossip also benefits the psyche of the target? Adults generally gossip about an absent third person, someone who isn't around to hear what people are saying about her or his behavior or lifestyle. In many cases, a comment may never get back to the target.

Children are different in this regard. They tend to gossip right in front of the target, often in the form of teasing. Though this may seem cruel, it also gives the victim an opportunity to know what others find offensive, silly, or nasty about his or her behavior or personal habits. How else can he or she stop?

Sociologist Gary Fine claims that children gossip practically from the time they learn to talk and to recognize other people.[36] In fact, gossip seems to play a central role in the conversations of four- and five-year-old children, and this role apparently does not diminish with age. Among older kids, gossip provides information that may be useful later, especially during adolescence: what happened on a date, who goes with whom, and who chickened out of a fight. Thus, talk provides a way for preadolescents to learn "the facts of life and the ways of the world" that they will later experience firsthand.

Like adults, children sometimes aim their gossip at powerful people—teachers and other authority figures in their lives. But children also aim downward toward marginal peers—the kid in the special class or the child who can't hit the ball and is constantly being chosen last for team sports.

Also like adults, many children are concerned that being the target of nasty gossip will damage their reputation. They also know, however, that their reputation will often protect them from gossip. For example, a well-liked homerun hitter on a Little League baseball team who blunders during a game will generally avoid criticism from his teammates. He may even be comforted by them. But let a kid hitting .150 commit the same error, and he is likely to be ignored, insulted, and gossiped about for the remainder of the season.

Even among adults, the sanctioning power of gossip is influenced by reputation or status. In every society, there are at least a few people who remain insulated from the negative consequences of talk because they either are powerful and wealthy or, at the other extreme, have a marginal status because of their poverty or bad reputation. In either case, such individuals can and do ignore or defy gossip, unlike those who are "in the middle of the social spectrum" and vulnerable to malicious talk.[37]

Individuals will often go to great lengths in order to present themselves in a favorable light and to avoid being humiliated in public. In the same way, individuals try to manage the information spread about them through gossip by transmitting flattering news about themselves and critical news about their opponents. In a competitive setting, for example, such as among employees vying for a promotion or students in an Ivy League school, gossip may be used to "put forward and protect their own interests and to attack their opponents in situations where open confrontation is too risky."[38]

The "stars" know the power of gossip in maintaining their celebrity status. It is true that some despise any form of publicity, even the most flattering. They tend to be celebrities who don't have to depend on public image in order to survive. For example, columnist Liz Smith was told a story about Jacqueline Onassis, who, after eating in a restaurant in New York City, complimented the chef on his granita and then asked him for the recipe. Thinking this was a charming but innocuous incident, Smith printed it in her column. Onassis's reaction was a surprise: "After it ran, she called the restaurant and complained bitterly: she was there as a private person, they shouldn't have given this information out, she didn't think it was right."[39]

To keep themselves in the public eye and memory, however, most Hollywood types go out of their way to seek publicity. In fact, they frequently hire expensive press agents. And these PR specialists frequently send planted gossip about their clients either to a particular columnist who "scoops" the competition or to local gossip columnists everywhere.

In some cases, a client will cooperate with a publicist by staging a newsworthy (or gossip-worthy) event strictly for the purpose of getting it into print. For example, Movie Star X is dating Movie Star Y for public consumption. Actually, they have quite different private relationships, but they date so they can get into the newspapers.

Everyday gossip may also be planted by the victim. Those who understand the psychology of gossip may make a defensive gesture designed to maintain some degree of control over what information and judgment become transmitted to others.

———— • ————

So far, we've looked at gossip that begins and ends in a single conversation. John tells Marsha about Fred's infidelity. Marsha has a bad memory for gossip, couldn't care less about what Fred does, or just isn't interested. So she never repeats the message and it dies—unless, of course, John has a good memory for gossip, cares a lot about what Fred does, or is intensely interested in juicy tidbits of gossip. Then, the conditions are right for gossip to become rumor, to go through the process we call the *rumor mill*, to be passed from person to person, and to get changed according to the desires or hostilities of those individuals who choose to pass it on. Gossip, then, is content, a message about people; rumor is a process. It takes a bit of gossip and reshapes it, modifies it in some way, and passes it along from individual to individual in different ways.

To the extent that gossip does become rumor, it may get distorted so much as to be unrecognizable from its original version. It is very much like the game telephone, in which a message is passed along (whispered) from one person to another until, by the fifth or sixth repeating, it has become thoroughly distorted. In the party version of the game, everyone laughs when the final version from the last person in the telephone chain is compared with the original.

In their classic work on the subject, psychologists Gordon Allport and Leo Postman suggested a model of rumor that was not very different from the party game we have just summarized.[40] They conceived of rumor as becoming more and more distorted as it passes in a straight line from one person to another. According to this "distortion" model, the following three processes are involved in the passing of a rumor: first, leveling—a rumor is shortened and told more concisely; second, sharpening—whatever is left of the rumor assumes greater importance and may be exaggerated; and third, assimilation—the rumor is changed so that it agrees more with the interests, personality, and expectations of the person telling it.

These stages in the transmission of a rumor can be seen in the communication of the following report: "Two boys and two girls were fishing when the boat in which they were riding overturned. Only the girls knew how to swim; they grabbed hold of the boys and guided them back to shore. Both boys were very grateful."

We have often given this story to our students as a demonstration of the distortion model of rumor. We ask our students to play telephone: to whisper the report to one another until it gets to the last student in the class, who writes it on a piece of paper and reads it to everyone else. The result often looks like this: "A boy and a girl are riding in a boat which overturns. Only the boy knows how to swim, so he saves the girl. She is very grateful." Thus, the final version of the rumor might have been predicted by Allport and Postman: It is shorter, focuses more on the act of one person saving another, and is wrong in an important respect: the boy is seen as saving the girl. Of course, what else would we expect?

Fredrick Koenig suggests, however, that rumors don't always work this way in everyday life.[41] First of all, we don't always pass a rumor in a straight line as in a classroom or a party game. In fact, we may pass it to many people all at once, who repeat it and send it around again. Think, for example, about a group of friends at a cocktail party. Do they usually sit or stand in a row? When someone spreads gossip, does he or she whisper it to one person at a time? Not usually. Instead, one person may bring an item of gossip to the entire group or to several members all at once. Discussing it together, they may find that other members have already heard the same thing, or they may offer evidence that the rumor is incorrect. Some may be skeptical; others may believe. A few may be totally indifferent to the whole thing and may refuse to join the discussion. Others may be so excited about what they hear that they immediately share it with their friends in other places.

In everyday life, rumor is a collective activity. The communication of a rumor often involves a number of specialized roles: messenger, interpreter, skeptic, auditor, and so on. In the transmission of one rumor—say, gossip about an affair between a teacher and her student—Joe might bring the message to his friends (Joe is the messenger), Alice might voice her disbelief (Alice plays the skeptic), and Jerry might remain unconcerned (Jerry is an auditor). In the next rumor, however,—say, an unconfirmed report that a large local employer will shortly lay off thousands of workers—Jerry may bring the message to his friends, and Alice and Joe may play the role of skeptics. Different people play different roles in different rumors.

The collective view of rumor has implications quite different from those envisaged by the distortion model. If people really pass rumors collectively, then the rumor can travel very fast to large numbers of listeners. In fact, the same person might expect to hear the same rumor, or some variation of it, from more than one source. Rumors travel back and forth, perhaps many times, through an entire network of people who know one another.

From this viewpoint, we cannot expect rumors necessarily to get shorter and more concise. Instead, they may pick up details, becoming elaborated, embellished, and exaggerated. Rumors may snowball into a much more elaborate version than the original. Indeed, if participants want to remain active in the process of transmitting a particular rumor, they will have to contribute something to expanding and modifying the message they receive (sometimes over and over again). This is how some rumors become distorted.[42]

An illustration of the snowballing of a rumor occurred in Orléans, France, a town of some 88,000 people located 110 kilometers south of Paris.[43] In early May 1969, adolescent girls in an Orléans high school began gossiping about a Jewish couple who owned and operated a local boutique.[44] The contemporary shop, called the Dorphée, sold contemporary dresses for girls and young women and did a thriving business. It was known for selling quality goods at competitive prices. There was a fitting room at the back of the shop and a workroom in the basement. These areas of the Dorphée figured prominently in the gossip that developed.

When the stories first began to circulate, they stated with confidence that two women had disappeared while shopping at the boutique. More specifically, the gossip suggested that the victims, while trying on clothes in the dressing room, had been given injections that rendered them unconscious. They were then carried downstairs to the cellar, where they were imprisoned while waiting to be sold into the white slave trade.

During the early stage of the gossip, talk about the disappearance of the two women was "authenticated." That is, the stories acquired the appearance of objective, factual information stemming from the most reliable sources in town. For example, the women who had disappeared were said to have been located in a particular place by the local authorities; the gossip specifically mentioned the "fact" that the police had found two drugged women in the Dorphée cellar. The women were then supposedly taken to the hospital, where they regained consciousness. In the gossip, this was also certified as coming from reliable sources, such as "The wife of one of the police told her neighbor." Interestingly, this gossip continued to flourish even though nothing about the alleged abductions was reported in the press and the police took no action against the supposed abductors. Moreover, the gossip made no effort to explain the silence of the press or the inaction of the police.

At first, the gossip mainly spread among teenage girls in the town. After a few weeks, however, it began to spill over into the adult community; girl told boy, pupil passed the story to teacher, and daughter told parents. The gossip was now circulating not only among groups of young people, but in families, offices, workshops, and factories as well. The story also spread to every social and economic group. Cleaning women talked to their wealthy employers, and middle-class housewives in the suburbs talked to one another.

The more the gossip spread, the more elaborate it became. The number of disappearances, which had begun as two, soon spiraled, with as many as sixty being cited, twenty-eight of which had vanished from the Dorphée alone. Nor was it any longer simply one shop that dealt in the white slave traffic, but an entire network of half a dozen stores, which were specifically named. In the stories, all the proprietors were Jewish except for the owners of the Alexandrine—newcomers to Orléans who had bought the store from its former Jewish owners. All the shops were modern and fashionable, catering to girls and young women. They all sold dresses with the exception of the Félix, a shoe store, where the drug was said to have been administered by means of a hypodermic syringe concealed in the heel of a shoe.

At this point in the evolution of the gossip, people in Orléans were beginning to worry. A number of teachers issued stern warnings to their students about these "dangerous shops," advising them to beware of "certain seductive advances." Some mothers forbade their daughters to set foot in these stores. By taking such protective measures, teachers and mothers inadvertantly lent their authority to the authentication of the gossip, thereby helping it to spread faster and further among the residents of Orléans.

As different versions of the story continued to circulate, their anti-Semitic potential increased. As part of the gossip, one would now hear comments like "Ah, these Jews." But at the same time, the gossip was now seen by some residents as totally unbelievable: "It's ridiculous . . . it's not possible . . . there are salesgirls around." Such objections did not stop the stories, however.

Boys and men seemed less open to the gossip, treating it as semifictional or as an old wives' tale. Although they rejected the stories as exaggeration, they often still accepted the accuracy of the original version; that is, they believed that a case of white slaving had actually occurred in a Jewish-owned store in town. The gossip's interest to them stemmed from its impropriety; they considered it a dirty story. Very few of the men felt that their wives or daughters were at any risk.

By May 23, Licht, the owner of Dorphée, had learned through a friend, whose daughter was in high school, that there was slanderous gossip being spread about him. Various local authorities, by this date, had also learned about the gossip, including the police department and the political parties. Yet none of these townspeople treated the story very seriously, thinking instead that it was merely a practical joke without validity. Their skepticism never turned into indignation that a false report about local residents was circulating without opposition. In a sense, their failure to act against the gossip may have helped to preserve it.

In the absence of any repressive measures, the gossip entered a new stage, in which it proliferated wildly. People in Orléans were now saying that the shops in question were all linked by secret underground tunnels, and that these tunnels met in a main sewer that flowed into the Loire, where a boat or a submarine would appear at night to pick up the abducted women. Also, more and more girls were disappearing, according to the gossip. Even the failure of the police to arrest the shopowners was explained in the latest stories: everyone had been bribed, including the police and the press.

By the end of May, the shopowners had begun to feel very threatened. Licht had received anonymous phone calls from people claiming to want "fresh meat" or addresses in Tangier. The victims of the gossip finally got together and appealed to the police for help, but they were told to wait until the following Monday—June 2—when the presidential elections would be over. On the next day, however, unruly crowds descended on the Orléans' marketplace. Housewives from the suburbs who believed the gossip came into town bursting with alarm and indignation. Crowds started forming outside the stores in question, severely reducing the number of customers who were willing to step inside. The few customers who dared enter the shops all had escorts. Licht expected the angry mob to break in at any moment.

The stir created by the latest gossip was met by direct opposition. For the first time, a counteroffensive was mounted. Two virulent articles were printed in local newspapers attacking the gossip as pure and utter fabrication. Formal statements of protest and condemnation appeared from local associations. It became increasingly difficult for the people of Orléans to take seriously the story that a group of Jewish white slavers was in control of everything—public institutions, political parties, and the press. There followed, then, a growing inclination to forget the whole episode, with more and more people now saying that they had never believed the gossip in the first place. In retrospective, they felt ridiculous.

Unlike the incident at Orléans, it is also possible for a rumor to remain essentially accurate, even though it is passed through a number of people. In the telephone model, a message is whispered from person to person. Nobody in the chain has an opportunity to discuss it or to have it repeated. In real life, however, such opportunities do indeed exist. As Koenig points out, everyday rumors rarely become garbled: "The teller talks plainly and wants to make sure the listener receives the message clearly. If the listener doesn't quite get the content, he or she will ask to have it repeated and the teller will do so eagerly."[45]

Before the Watergate hearings in the 1970s, for example, rumors about President Nixon's role in covering up the break-in of the offices used by the Democratic National Committee circulated widely by word of mouth, television news reports, and radio talk shows. By the time of Nixon's resignation from office, most of these rumors had been unequivocally confirmed, despite their widespread circulation.

In the midst of panic, we would not, of course, expect a great deal of accuracy in communicating a rumor. At the extreme, nightclub customers might get trampled to death because someone incorrectly shouts, "Fire." Or the same nightclub customers might burn to death believing wrongly that a warning over the public address system is part of a comedian's routine (something like this actually happened on May 28, 1977, at the Beverly Hills Supper Club in Kentucky; 164 burned to death).

The ability of people to evaluate critcally a rumor seems to remain intact as long as their collective tension and excitement do not run wild. When things don't get entirely out of hand, rumors spread on the basis of plausibility rather than emotion.[46]

Thus, in everyday life, some rumors may actually become more accurate and valid as they are passed along from person to person. Take, for example, an individual who approaches a rumor with a critical set. If he is well informed and able to verify the authenticity of the story, he may also be able to eliminate invalid or irrelevant details or at least to maintain its essential integrity. In the game of telephone, there is motivation only to make sure a story is passed, whether or not it is true. In everyday life, however, people who pass rumors may be extremely motivated to pass an accurate account of what they have been told by others.[47]

Under what conditions does gossip become rumor? It is more likely to spread when events are ambiguous and anxiety-laden, and when a target is socially connected. For example, gossip about a well-known local politician whose wife has been killed under mysterious circumstances stands a good chance of spreading throughout the local community. The politician in question is connected to many people in town; murder makes people uneasy; and a suspect has not yet been charged or arrested. People will talk. By contrast, gossip about an obscure recluse who has been arrested for shoplifting will be quickly dead-ended. After all, nobody knows him, nobody cares very much, and nobody feels confused.

Ambiguous situations often provide the context for gossip that circulates beyond its original source. Wherever facts are undetermined or in conflict, where there is uncertainty about the present and the future, gossip is likely to flourish.

Psychologist Ralph Rosnow has shown that rumors about other people are especially likely to fill the conversations of individuals who are anxious or nervous about what is happening to them. Psychologists have discovered, in fact, that individuals who score high on the Taylor Manifest Anxiety Scale—a measure of anxiety—are especially likely to spread gossip and rumor.[48]

This is not to argue that gossip always reduces anxiety. In fact, instead of exorcising anxiety, it may work in reverse. There are times when stories that we hear circulating about our friends, family, or neighbors confirm our greatest fears. People really do commit acts of infidelity, promiscuity, vandalism, and dishonesty. People actually do get separated and divorced, drink too much at a party, or have trouble with their children. And sometimes we hear about it.

When the same anxiety is shared by several people, then they will all gossip together in an attempt to explain their situation. Where food shortages exist, people gossip about distribution and gift giving;[49] where access to economic resources depends on tracing descent through uncertain genealogies, people gossip about one another's ancestors, real and imagined;[50] where witchcraft is a cultural belief, people gossip about who is and is not a witch.[51]

For the same reason, an office grapevine is strengthened by a bad economy: when workers are being laid off, when there is talk that the company may be sold, when there are signs that the management will change, or when a member of the staff is seen spending a lot of time with the boss. The possibility of change makes people nervous.

Under such conditions, employees seek to define an ambiguous, anxiety-laden situation; they attempt to locate the source of their economic woes and place the blame. The result is widespread gossip about employees who sleep with the boss to maintain their jobs, about payoffs and kickbacks, about people on the payroll who don't deserve to be there, about potential new owners, about the ruthlessness of a banker whose last name sounds Jewish, or about the inequities inherent in affirmative action for blacks and women.

Employees gossip to explain a situation that they don't understand, one that might have a direct and personal impact on their own lives. They spread news where none exists. Sometimes the gossip only misleads and mis-informs; at other times, however, it helps clarify. Psycho-logically, all feel better because they believe they have figured out something that didn't make sense before. Hav-ing some understanding gives everybody a sense of control over her or his life.

Outside the office, anxieties that affect almost everyone involve illness, disaster, or death. Consequently, much of our everyday gossip and rumor deal with these topics. On a national level, a number of celebrities have been widely reported to have died in the face of over-whelming evidence to the contrary—including their per-sonal denials. In 1969, a rumor took hold that Paul McCartney had been killed in an automobile accident and had been replaced by a double. As the story of McCartney's death gained momentum, his fans discovered more and more clues to support their erroneous suspicions. Some claimed to hear messages of death ("I buried Paul") when their Beatles albums were played backward and the back-ground noise was filtered out. Others found visual images of Paul's death on the album covers of "Sgt. Pepper," "Abbey Road," and "The Magical Mystery Tour." Still other fans discovered that when the picture of McCartney on the cover of *Life* magazine was held up to a strong light, a car from the ad on the reverse side was superimposed across his chest.[52]

Since the McCartney gossip, a number of other celebrities have been falsely pronounced dead before their time. Otherwise known as the Beaver of "Leave It To Bea-ver" fame, Jerry Mathers was repeatedly rumored to have died in the Vietnam War. His activities as a businessman and part-time actor in Hollywood didn't seem to convince those gossip addicts who were certain he had been killed in combat. Another example can be found in the widely circulated gossip during the closing years of the 1970s that little, lovable Mikey, who starred for a long time in the Life cereal commercials, had perished while eating a carbonated candy that exploded in his stomach.

In a popular reversal of death gossip, there have also been stories that famous people thought to be dead are actually very much alive. To this day, as we noted earlier, certain people remain convinced that Adolph Hitler is alive and living under an assumed name in Argentina. Some continue to believe that President John Kennedy was never really killed in Dallas and, to this day, remains in hiding. Gossip continues to circulate, especially among youthful, second-generation fans of the rock group called the Doors, that their lead singer, Jim Morrison, didn't succumb to a drug overdose as popularly believed, and that he is actually making records under a different name.

We can learn a great deal about the spread of exaggerated, if not erroneous, gossip by examining the reaction to a recent disaster in the Soviet Union. In April 1986, the Soviet Union announced to the world that a nuclear accident had damaged an atomic reactor at its Chernobyl power plant in the Ukraine. Radiation levels reportedly ten times above normal swept across Denmark, Finland, and Sweden, more than 750 miles away.

American newspapers reported that the explosion and meltdown at Chernobyl had left "more than 2,000 people dead and thousands more suffering radiation sickness." Days later, these press reports suggested that fires of tremendous intensity continued to engulf the nuclear plant and that destruction of major proportions had occurred. By May 1, however, the smoke was beginning to clear and the actual dimensions of the Chernobyl disaster were becoming more visible. Chernobyl had been a tremendous disaster for the Soviet people and their neighbors, but it had claimed far fewer lives than reported by the Western press. In fact, there were only two, rather than two thousand, deaths, at least in the first few days following the explosion (thirty-one had lost their lives by August 1986). In response, Moscow's state-controlled television charged that the Western press had mounted a campaign of "slanderous inventions" about the Chernobyl situation.[53]

How could such a large discrepancy have occurred? Is it conceivable that the U.S. government or media actually exploited the tragedy for propaganda purposes by intentionally inflating the proportions of the disaster? Had propagandists at the U.S. Information Agency (USIA) deliberately exaggerated the dimensions of the Soviet nuclear accident?

We may never know for sure, though the idea certainly crossed the minds of propagandists in the West. A letter, later declared to be fraudulent, was sent in the aftermath of the Chernobyl disaster—a letter in which a "USIA agent" advocated encouraging our allies in Europe to spread false reports that the Soviet disaster had claimed two thousand to three thousand lives and threatened the nations of Europe with widespread nuclear contamination. U.S. Information Agency officials insisted that their agency had made no effort to encourage such rumors and that the letter was a hoax.[54]

Whatever the reaction of Western propaganda experts, the initial cause of these exaggerated estimates of death and destruction can be traced directly to official secrecy in the Soviet Union. Queries by the Swedes regarding abnormally high levels of radiation were met with Soviet denials and silence. For nine days, details of the disaster at Chernobyl were withheld from the world press. It was the following weekend before a Soviet official even began to give a straightforward account.[55]

By then, it was simply too late to stem the tide of exaggerated rumor. Fearful of being victimized by radiation, the world waited anxiously for official sources to define the situation. When formal news was not forthcoming, however, word-of-mouth reports gained credibility. Ironically, the capacity of the Soviet government to control information was largely responsible for leaving a vacuum of news, which, in turn, was quickly filled by rumors of mass death and destruction. One can only imagine the network of everyday gossip that must have developed among citizens of the Eastern European countries, whose physical safety was immediately imperiled but who received little in the way of official information.

The key elements of secrecy and anxiety found in world reaction to this nuclear accident have been seen before in Soviet public relations. In fact, these same elements have on occasion generated a good deal of gossip depicting Soviet leaders as frail, sickly, on the verge of death, or worse. Whether or not Western propagandists encouraged such reports is a matter of speculation.

Leonid Brezhnev succeeded Nikita Krushchev as chief of the Soviet party in 1964. By 1968, there were widespread reports in the Western press that he was "mildly ill," and that he had suffered a spell of "faintness."[56]

In 1970, the press was reporting rumors that Brezhnev was suffering from high blood pressure and that "possible changes in the Soviet leadership were imminent."[57] By 1972, reports of the sixty-four-year-old Brezhnev's illness had escalated. After an unexplained absence of one month, he was said to walk slowly and carefully, and to have lost weight and color. His health problems, it was rumored, could be traced back to 1961, when he had suffered from a "heart ailment."[58]

Another unexplained absence from public view in 1974 prompted speculation that the Soviet leader had "influenza." Reporters noted that he looked "drawn and haggard."[59] Again, a year later, Brezhnev retreated from public affairs. When he reappeared after two months, there were reports that he had been "seriously ill." In his first public speech after returning, reporters said that he pronounced his words "indistinctly," lending credibility to reports that "he had been undergoing treatment for an ailment involving his left jaw or his throat." In response, Soviet officials claimed that he had had the flu. When asked about the state of his health, Brezhnev told reporters that he felt fine, "as surely you can see."[60] Six weeks later, new speculation about his health appeared in public when the Soviet leader walked out of a dinner before the main course was served.[61]

Later that year, the press suggested, after he postponed a scheduled talk with the visiting French president, that Brezhnev might have cancer and that his health might be deteriorating badly. Reporters noted, however, that he looked "healthy and energetic."[62]

Nineteen seventy-six was a good year for Brezhnev, at least in Western press reports. Still, articles about Soviet-American relations voiced concern about the state of his health—specifically, whether he suffered from emphysema as a result of heavy smoking, jaw problems, a bad heart, and a chronic bronchial condition. To reporters, his jaw seemed to droop, and he sometimes stumbled over words in his speech, although he also "seemed fit, vigorous, and rested." In January, unnamed U.S. officials told the press that an agreement on limiting bombers and missles might hinge on whether the Soviet leader "retained his political and physical health in the months ahead."[63]

Western press accounts of Brezhnev's health became increasingly negative in 1977, after the Soviet General Secretary reached his seventieth birthday. Reporters claimed that he looked "considerably aged, his cheeks puffed and his voice raspy," perhaps as a result of jaw and dental problems. "Western intelligence officials" described Brezhnev as having serious health problems, though no terminal illness. His problems were said to include a cardiovascular problem, a jaw problem, a worsening hearing problem, obesity, poor eyesight, and overmedication accounting for his fatigue and slurred speech.[64] After Brezhnev inexplicably canceled some important public appearances, a Japanese news agency reported that the Soviet envoy to Japan had told the Japanese foreign minister that the Soviet president had been discharged from a hospital, where he was recovering from an undisclosed illness.[65]

Throughout the remainder of his term in office, until his death in 1982, news reports continued to depict Brezhnev's health as failing. His face and neck were said to be swollen and pallid, and he walked in a stiff, mechanical manner. He may have had difficulty breathing and showed signs of strain.[66] Unexplained postponements of important meetings with national leaders were once again blamed by unnamed Western sources on Brezhnev's poor health. American intelligence officials claimed that he had emphysema, gout, leukemia, and an irregular heartbeat controlled by a pacemaker. Anonymous French sources told reporters that he also suffered from occasional lapses of memory and attention.[67]

In April 1982, Western newspapers reported rumors that Brezhnev had been hospitalized for an undisclosed illness. Running true to form, Soviet officials would neither confirm nor deny the speculation.[68] One week later, the Soviet Foreign Ministry's press department stated that the seventy-five-year-old Soviet leader was on a "routine winter vacation," not in a hospital.

Seven months later, on November 11, the state-controlled television in Moscow announced that Leonid I. Brezhnev, the Soviet leader for eighteen years, had died the day before. The announcer gave no indication of the cause of death.[69]

We will probably never determine with certainty whether Brezhnev's state of health was as dire as depicted in Western press reports. What we can conclude, however, is that inadequate news from official Soviet sources accounted for the large amount of attention given to Brezhnev's health by the Western press. A lack of information also accounted for the reliance of Western reporters on unnamed intelligence sources that may have had a vested interest in depicting the Soviet leader as sickly and frail. Whether between countries or between neighbors, gossip is a predictable response to secrecy in the face of anxiety about world events.

## Chapter 3    THE GOSSIP REPORTER AS ANTHROPOLOGIST

Anthropologists attempt to understand life in other cultures as well as in their own. They travel the four corners of the globe, pen and tape recorder in hand, hoping to uncover the details of little-known tribal rites and customs. Gossip reporters really aren't so different. Like anthropologists, they try to get the "inside scoop" on celebrity culture by examining what the "natives" of Hollywood do at work and at leisure, on the set and at home, while attending dinner parties or business meetings.

Anthropologists are, of course, considered objective scientists who gather knowledge for the sake of knowledge, whereas gossip columnists and reporters are widely seen as motivated more by fame and wealth than by a search for truth. In the public image, anthropologists are evenhanded, accurate and ethical, whereas gossip reporters are nasty and unethical in terms of both what they print and how they secure their information. Indeed, they are seen as powerful figures whose printed gossip can harm if not destroy the careers of celebrities. This is the image, but what is the reality?

Looking at the lives of legendary columnists active in the first half of this century, one finds a certain degree of reality in this image.[1] They did indeed exercise a great deal of power and could influence the careers of the stars.

From the very beginning, Louella Parsons dominated gossip about the movie industry. She came to Hollywood in 1925, where she enjoyed a virtual monopoly on celebrity news. Her syndicated gossip column was the first and, for a time, the only one in town. So if you were a big-name Hollywood movie star or ever hoped to be, you really had to deal with Louella. She had the power to make or break an actor by giving or withholding publicity. She could also snap the career of a Hollywood press agent like a twig. Many publicists phoned her on a daily basis to offer a newsworthy tidbit about a client or just to beg for mercy.

The experience of Thomas Wood, a Hollywood press agent, illustrates the tight grip that Louella had on the celebrity scene and the potential she possessed for unethical conduct. In 1939, Wood wrote an article in the *Saturday Evening Post* which was highly critical of her. He suggested, for example, that "Even in her own field, where bad writing is as natural and as common as breathing, Louella's stands out like an asthmatic's gasps."[2] According to Wood, as soon as his story was in print, he became the victim of "a kind of blacklisting" by Louella, who informed everyone who was anything in the industry of her disdain for him. For the next fifteen years, Woods had a lot of trouble finding work.[3]

During the 1930s, the doom-and-gloom atmosphere of the Great Depression had fans flocking to the movies in record numbers to see such silver-screen idols as Jean Harlow, Ginger Rogers, James Cagney, Edward G. Robinson, James Stewart, and Clark Gable. The same need for "escapist fare" that spawned Hollywood heroes also generated an increased readership for Hollywood gossip.

It was therefore inevitable that Louella's monopoly would be challenged. In 1938, a has-been, over-the-hill actress, Hedda Hopper, began writing her own version of Hollywood gossip, which millions of Americans read on a daily basis. At about the same time a former chorus girl from London named Sheilah Graham entered the struggle for Hollywood power and influence. She stayed for thirty-two years, writing a gossip column that, while lacking the absolute authority of Louella Parsons or Hedda Hopper never lacked in biting criticism. Of Errol Flynn, she gossiped, "He says he doesn't worry about money just as long as he can reconcile his net income with his gross habits."[4]

By 1940, Walter Winchell's gossip column was carried by more than a thousand papers, and his combined radio and newspaper audience exceeded fifty million. He helped to "make" stars like Frank Sinatra; he also "banished" celebrities from his column.[5] After a critical article about Winchell appeared in the *New Yorker*, he swore revenge against its editor, Harold Ross. In one of his columns, Winchell alleged that Ross didn't wear underwear. As though this weren't enough, Winchell also used his influence to have Ross banned from the prestigious Stork Club.

Winchell also used his considerable power against those individuals in the entertainment industry who criticized him. In his attack on Lyle Stuart, editor of *Exposé*, Winchell was fed "dirt" about Stuart from the New York City Police Department, which was printed in Winchell's column. Stuart was eventually forced by this bad publicity to leave his position as a journalist. Similarly, radio talk-show host Barry Gray suffered from Winchell's angry words about him. For three years, the columnist kept up a vicious campaign of gossip against Gray which led the Broadway crowd to shun him. Sponsors soon dropped Gray's program, and for a period of time, he lost two television shows.

But even among the most notorious of gossip columnists, cases of unethical revelation and distortion are the exception to the rule. Contrary to the popular image, early columnists rarely revealed facts that would have destroyed a star. Not unlike anthropologists, these professional gossips worked according to a code of ethics that, though not always observed, frequently served to determine what would and would not get into print.

Some may have seen Louella Parsons as a ruthless, cold-blooded gossipmonger, but from her point of view, she adhered to a strict system of ethics regarding what to print and how to secure information. She claimed never to have broken a confidence or to have used an off-the-record remark. Moreover, she denied with some pride ever printing blind items, which sounded juicy enough but could not be verified. In her own words, "I've kept secrets and watched others profit from my keeping them. I've covered up infidelities and scandals and then seen them publicly proclaimed, frequently by the protagonist himself."[6]

Walter Scott, whose "Personality Parade" appears weekly in *Parade* magazine, suggests that a revelation of homosexuality during the early years of Hollywood could have severely harmed an actor's reputation. According to Scott, the Hollywood studio often played a major role in hiding the sexual orientation of such actors as Rock Hudson, Montgomery Clift, Tyrone Power, Charles Laughton, James Dean, Ramon Navarro, and Sal Mineo. Although these stars were eventually known in the movie colony as "gay deceivers," their reputations never made the daily newspaper or the scandal magazine. Gossip columnists and reporters joined in this "conspiracy of silence" because they realized these actors would never work again if the truth about their sexuality became public. Even the sleaziest publications cooperated in their own way by striking a deal with a studio to kill a harmful story. For example, an article about actor Rory Calhoun's prison record was given to *Confidential Magazine* by Universal-International studios to get the magazine to drop another story about the homosexuality of one of its more important star performers. *Confidential* printed the piece about Calhoun but eliminated the story about the gay star.

Columnist James Brady is uncomfortable writing what he calls "pillow talk" about the private lives of celebrities. As an example, Brady recalls an episode during his days at *Women's Wear Daily* when Senator Eugene McCarthy was still an important political figure in the country. Brady received a phone call from McCarthy the day after they ran a piece revealing that the Senator and his wife had separated. Brady recalls, "I had to read it to him over the phone. And, it was a sad voice at the other end. When it was over, I said, 'Well, Senator, that's it.' And he said, 'Well, you were gentle with us and it could have been worse, but you still don't like to hear it, do you?' I felt terrible, even though the story was accurate."[7]

Many of today's columnists continue to reject vicious gossip. Brady, for example, avoids labeling a celebrity as a homosexual or a lesbian who has not volunteered that information. He also dislikes writing about marriages breaking up, especially if children are involved. He refuses to reveal anyone's sexual perversions, heterosexual or otherwise. Instead, Brady prefers what he calls "power gossip"—"who's getting hired, who's getting fired, which big deal may be next in the works, what movie script is falling apart because the guy can't get a hold of the characters, and so on."

Like their counterparts at daily newspapers, tabloid editors consider items of gossip in terms of the overall image they convey to their readers. According to Janet Charlton of the *Star*, her editor sometimes rejects a story when he feels that it crosses the fine line between what is "a little goofy, funny, or offbeat" and what is "vulgar." The following item about Boy George was considered "in bad taste" by Janet's editor and therefore never appeared in her column:

> Boy George went to a bar in Holywood where he had a real hard time. First, he had a fight with this drunk girl at the bar. He ended up throwing a drink in her face and slapping her. And before the evening was over, a real drunk guy walked up to Boy George and threw up on his shoes. Boy George had a fit. He went into the men's room and said it was so filthy he refused to use it. Instead, he used the lady's room to wash up.

*Enquirer* founder and chairman Generoso Pope maintains that the official policy of his paper is not to print sordid or off-color stories about celebrities. "There are certain types of celebrity stories that we won't touch," says Pope. "We will not touch anything of a sexual nature. No sex stories. We will not go after any type of sordid story involving celebrities' children. We will not touch homosexual stories involving celebrities unless something has broken in the national press. And if we do do anything on it then we very much water it down. We want people to be able to take it home and not be afraid if their children read it."

Certain topics do indeed seem to be regarded as off-limits by a number of tabloid reporters. Just as for columnists who write gossip for daily newspapers, the most prominent of taboo topics in leading tabloids are homosexuality and drug addiction. According to *Enquirer* reporter Richard Taylor, these are probably the very characteristics that are prominent in the lifestyles of Hollywood stars. Yet these are also the two stories the tabloids won't touch: "First of all, you can't prove it; and, second, who wants to read it anyway?"

*People* magazine also does not print everything it knows. "There's a joke around this building," says Hal Wingo, its assistant managing editor, "that we produce two magazines every week—one we can print and one we can't. You learn a lot more about people in the process of doing this work than you can use, and in some cases, that would be right to use."

According to Wingo, homosexuality is never mentioned in *People*, although occasionally stories are run about celebrities hooked on drugs or alcohol. As revealing as they may be, such stories are written with the cooperation of the celebrity whose addiction is being made public. For instance, MacKenzie Phillips from "One Day at a Time" was nudged into doing a story in *People* after she entered a drug rehabilitation program. So was Betty Ford after she dried out from her alcoholism in a Palm Springs clinic.

How does the gossip reporter's system of ethics translate into content? Given the reputation of columnists for spreading the dirt, it is perhaps surprising that gossip columns have for decades actually tended to print flattering, favorable information about celebrities.[8] Many of their activities, both in and out of professional roles, have received explicit approval from the professional gossips; for example, Ginger Rogers receiving a standing ovation for her performance in a new Broadway play or Danny Kaye being applauded for his performance in a new film. Hy Gardner called Carol Channing's new position "well-deserved," and Earl Wilson praised the hospitality of Buddy Hackett's wife at a party she had given.

More recently, Marilyn Beck suggested that Jessica Lange "could turn out to be the dark-horse winner of the best-actress race" for her role in *Sweet Dreams*; James Brady called Dan Greenburg's latest book "typically hilarious"; Frank Swertlow referred to Oprah Winfrey as "TV's hottest schmoozer"; and Larry King's column in *USA Today* called Mary Higgins Clark's novel "wonderful."

The regional columns also publish positive gossip. For example, columnist Gerald Kloss in the *Milwaukee Journal* reported that Sally Struthers was happy to be working again on a weekly series, "Nine to Five." Struthers claimed, "It's a way to hold down a steady job and be a decent mother at the same time." Hanania, Gillespie, and Siewers in the *Chicago Sun-Times* wrote that Bill Johnson, the star "maniac" of the *Texas Chainsaw Massacre* movies, is actually a nice guy in real life. The six-foot-two, 280-pound Johnson likes to play bridge and plant flowers at his Austin, Texas, home.

The tendency of gossip columnists to make flattering references to celebrities does not go unnoticed among the columnists themselves. Some express concern about being perceived as too kind, flattering, and complimentary. As one columnist put it,

> What really bothers me is what somebody said last night, "Oh, you only write nice things about people." Well, I don't think so. I mean, Senator John Kerry was very pissed off when I wrote that he no longer had residence in Boston. I don't think the head of John Hancock was too happy when I wrote about his divorce; I don't think Joe Perry was too happy when he heard he was being sued. It's a terrible insult to say to a gossip columnist that she only writes nice things!

When a celebrity's disapproved behavior does appear in a gossip column, it almost never represents a violation of the major norms of society. Felonious criminal activities are virtually nonexistent; for example, gangster connections never get reported. Instead, the disapproved activities are usually minor infractions of everyday rules. Similarly, anthropologists often focus on the small rules of a community, on the folkways that make everyday life possible. They describe everything from cosmetic mutilation, unusual diets and eating arrangements, clothing, and work habits to dating rituals.

For at least the last forty years, syndicated columnists have focused on folkways, not mores, on eccentricity rather than evil. In earlier years, it was Catherine Deneuve announcing that she would pose nude for *Playboy*

magazine; Lady Churchill putting her foot through a paint-
ing that she disliked; Redd Foxx refusing to attend his
daughter's wedding because his estranged wife had
excluded his name from the invitation; Martha Ray osten-
tatiously displaying her mink stole; or Kay Ballard "mis-
behaving" on a movie set. More recently, columnists Sneed
and O'Malley in the *Chicago Tribune* claimed that Prince
Charles tried to cover up his enlarging baldspot at Prince
Andrew's wedding. Marge Crumbaker of the *Houston Post*
noted that Ben Vereen was upset when many of the people
in the audience of his recent play left at intermission, never
to return. Herb Caen of the *San Francisco Chronicle*
announced that I. Magnin had objected to a local store
calling itself I. Magnet (the store is now Magnet P.I.).

Into the 1980s, gossip columns continue to print
"media small talk." For example, Janet Charlton's column,
"Star People," in the *Star* contains a number of offbeat,
semihumorous stories about the everyday idiosyncracies
and frivolities of Hollywood celebrities. She rarely criti-
cizes a star for a major transgression or blunder. In a recent
column, Charlton wrote about Zsa Zsa Gabor's arriving at
a Hollywood supermarket "dressed to kill in diamonds
and a fur coat" only to purchase the least expensive generic
items like hot dogs and paper towels. Charlton also reported
that teen idol Madonna was a "popcorn fanatic" who
arranged to have jars of her favorite brand of popcorn and
a popper flown to four locations in the Orient during the
filming of her new motion picture.

*People* cover stories reveal what the magazine considers not only appropriate but essential to print.[9] Almost
always, the cover depicts a celebrity, most often from show
business, sometimes from politics, and infrequently from
science, journalism, education, business, or the law. In

1983–1985, for example, *People* cover stories highlighted television personalities like Pierce Brosnan, Tom Selleck, Joan Rivers, and Linda Evans; motion picture stars like Natalie Wood, Bo Derek, Dolly Parton, and Paul Newman; and musicians like Paul McCartney, Karen Carpenter, Michael Jackson, and Cyndi Lauper. But they also featured Dr. Ruth, Geraldine Ferraro, Ted Kennedy, Diane Sawyer, and Prince Charles, and they did covers on teen suicide, the Korean airline tragedy, and Live Aid.

Although the cover stories may involve an area of some seriousness, *People* leads its readers to happy or hopeful conclusions. For example, after having problems with his personal life and career, Chevy Chase is doing well now with a new baby daughter and a hit movie, *Vacation*; Barbra Streisand discusses her movie *Yentl*, her relationship with her father, and hope for the future; Michael Jackson survives a bizarre accident (his hair caught on fire) and adds another chapter to his life story; his autobiography is being edited by Jackie Onassis; Boy George is helping to lead show business's newest trend toward "gender blend"; Cyndi Lauper has overcome bad times and bankruptcy to emerge as rock's new video queen.

Unlike *People*, one of the most important reasons for the incredible success of the *National Enquirer* is its reliance on the medium of television. Who watches what on TV determines much of the content of this popular tabloid, according to celebrity reporter Sam Rubin. He claims that the *Enquirer* would prefer to feature an actor who appears regularly on television, even if he doesn't play a major role, rather than some big-name Hollywood star who does a movie once a year.

The more frequently celebrities appear on the tube, the easier it is for members of the audience to identify with them. For lonely people, TV actors become friends or buddies and receive tremendous amounts of mail; their fans adore them and want to know what happens behind the scenes, in everyday life. For this reason, actors who appear in daytime soap operas may be regarded by tabloid reporters as more desirable than even prime-time performers. After all, soap operas are on the air five days a week, Monday through Friday, not just weekly.

Celebrities apparently don't have to do very much to get into a supermarket tabloid.[10] Their presence is almost always a result of some minor or mundane event: a quarrel between spouses, the early stages of a romance, or a shopping spree. In a single issue of a particular tabloid, for example, there were articles about Johnny Carson's divorce, Steven Ford's preference for living away from the city, how Bjorn Borg's wife saved their marriage, and Dolly Parton's fear of having throat problems. The major tabloids have run stories about Roger Daltrey, the curly-headed star of the rock group The Who, because he owns a chain of cut-rate hardware stores; about the late John Wayne's preference not to let anyone see him without his toupee; about the Plexiglas paperweight that President Reagan keeps on his desk; about tough-guy Roger Moore, who is a wimp in real life; and about Bea Arthur from television's "Golden Girls," who insisted on going barefoot at a Hollywood premier when her feet started hurting her. Just as in syndicated gossip columns, few celebrities who appear in tabloids are featured because of a major achievement or violation of a major norm (i.e., committing a felony).

Occasionally, thorny personal problems in the lives of celebrities are described. Hollywood stars and big-name political figures suffer from divorce and separation, infidelity, premarital pregnancy, and arguments between spouses. Relatively few of the articles about them deal directly with the films they are acting in, their new television series, their appearance on the Broadway stage, or their election to the Senate. Almost none portrays them as remarkable or outstanding. When it comes to celebrities, tabloid readers apparently want (or are perceived to want) gossip about their private lives rather than their "on stage" successes. Readers want to "get to know" the celebrities outside their professional roles and as human beings with human qualities.

In contrast to that of celebrities, the appearance of ordinary people is uniformly a result of an extraordinary achievement, an exceptional quality, an act of heroism, an unusual talent, or a miraculous occurrence. Like anthropologists who witness ordinary members of a tribe or primitive society running barefoot across hot coals, swinging from poles with large fishhooks through their backs, drinking water from a sacred well that has the power to make barren women fertile, or engaging in spirit possessions and exorcisms, tabloid reporters describe amazing things in the lives of normal people.

For example, many articles describe everyday people performing great acts of generosity or kindness: Diane and Frank Pollin of Spokane, Washington, adopted a sixty-seven-year-old dwarf when they heard that she was being sent to a nursing home. After a Florida man saved eight-foot-tall Bigfoot from being shot, the big hairy beast not only saved the same man from drowning but also fought off a pack of wild dogs chasing the man's son.

Other articles examine bravery or courage in the face of personal hardship. At eighty-one, Beulah Harrison shattered her pelvis and hip. Doctors told her she might never walk again. Within four years, however, Beulah's remarkable determination led her to fifteen dance championships, winning prizes for the cha-cha, the waltz, the fox trot, the tango, and the rumba. Sue Docker was pulled out to sea by a powerful current off the coast of Australia. She managed to stay afloat for forty-four hours in shark-infested waters, despite thirst, exhaustion, and exposure. Finally, she was washed ashore on a small island and wrote the word *help* in three-foot letters in the sand. After she had been given up for dead, a helicopter spotted her message, landed, and flew her to the nearest hospital.

Miracles are sometimes the focal point of tabloid stories. Giuseppe Pinetti of Italy can make crucifixes bleed. As soon as he touches a crucifix, Type A blood appears from the chest of the image. Giuseppe is being hailed as a new saint because the blood he produces from crosses apparently cures all kinds of diseases, from psoriasis to ulcers. Clarence Washburn and Dean Ploth were coming in for a landing when their plane developed instrument trouble. Two miles from the end of the runway, power lines loomed ahead of them. Flying on reduced power, Ploth could not avoid the lines, skimmed the wires, slid to a screeching halt, and suddenly somersaulted upside-down. The plane dangled precariously on wires charged with 220,000 volts of electricity ninety feet above the ground, hanging only by its propeller and landing gear. The two men were finally rescued unharmed. While a man was sleeping in his Boston apartment, a gas explosion blew him out of the building. Amazingly, he traveled from the building's fourth floor to ground level without falling out of bed or getting a scratch.

Ordinary people are frequently depicted as having extraordinary abilities or talents. Peggy Grant, twenty-six, is a five-foot, eleven-inch, 210-pound woman who's been busted for shoplifting at least thirteen times since 1977. Known to local police as "Jaws," she clamps her teeth on the hard plastic sensors attached to clothing to catch shoplifters and snaps them off as if they were made of soft bread slices. Recently, Peggy was busy chomping away on a plastic sensor in a dressing room only to be discovered by a clerk who heard loud crunching noises. Doron Blake was the first baby conceived by artificial insemination to be brilliant. Only four months after his birth, little Doron was already conducting Mozart and Chopin, was drinking straight from a glass, and had started playing the piano. First tests on Doron showed that he might have an IQ as high as 200.

Strange medical problems plague otherwise normal people. Evelyn Muxart walked around for almost two weeks with a bullet in her head without knowing it—or that her husband had shot her while she slept. Only after she complained of migraines and fainted at work did Evelyn realize what had happened.

Gossip often capitalizes on irony: a gap between what we expect of others and what we discover about them, between their reputations and their actual behavior. Historically, for example, French kings were expected to have mistresses, so their sexual affairs did not make the best material for gossipmongers of the day. But twentieth-century mayors are not expected to have mistresses—especially when the mayor is Catholic and flaunts his illicit sexual activities by driving his mistress around in his car. That's what made Mayor Jimmy Walker become ex-Mayor Jimmy Walker.[11]

The same principle applies to obscure individuals. Thus, people are less likely to gossip about the sexual activities of a prostitute than about those of an otherwise conventional, middle-class married woman who sneaks off in the dead of night to have affairs with her lovers. The gap between reputation and actual behavior can also be seen in the attractiveness of positive gossip. Donating a large sum of money to charity is less likely to be gossiped about when the money is contributed by a clean-cut type than by a hooker. We expect prostitutes to have sex with many different men; we do not expect them to donate large sums of money to charity. This irony is frequently what makes gossip interesting.

Perhaps this irony explains why so many of the tabloid articles detailing the fantastic accomplishments or adventures of obscure individuals focus on behavior which is apparently inconsistent with what we might expect in everyday life. For example, Gerrie met Magdalena at a local disco; they danced, fell in love, and were married shortly thereafter. She was a sixty-two-year-old great-grandmother and he was a twenty-two-year-old. On his wedding day, Gerrie became the instant great-grandfather of a six-month old baby boy, and seven of his new stepchildren were older than he was.

These cases are far from unique. Everyday in the tabloids, you can find unexpected phenomena, such as "Woman Preacher Is Nation's Top Jockey," "Genius with Earthshaking IQ Works as Belly Dancer," and "Alligator Man and Monkey Girl Happily Wed for 45 Years." In the tabloid version of everyday people, anything can happen—and usually does.

Even when they portray the unexpected, and the ironic, gossip tabloids communicate an important positive message, despite their reputation for printing gross and gory material. Overall, they strongly suggest that happiness may be just around the corner, if not already present, for the average person. True, a minority of the people who are featured have difficult if not impossible problems, but these are more likely to be rich and famous individuals whose money and status have not guaranteed them happiness and contentment. Indeed, the majority of targets of gossip—and especially the ordinary, obscure types—are capable of satisfactory if not extraordinary accomplishments. Miracles can and do happen to them. Everyday life is worthwhile and exciting, even for the "little" people of the world, and the world of celebrities is not so great after all.

The positive message found in gossip tabloids seems well represented in other forms of popular culture, including popular song lyrics, movie themes, and situation comedies on prime-time television. Many observers have noted that popular culture or mass entertainment fails to educate its audience and encourages escapism or false consciousness. In this sense, the gossip tabloid may be just as much an agent of control as its more negative counterpart in scandalous small talk. The *National Enquirer* may reinforce the status quo by presenting its readers with issue after issue of trivia or hype, by discouraging discontent and protest, and by supporting prevailing norms and values. Apparently, this is precisely the message that some ten million readers want to hear.

There is another payoff for the readers as well. They can feel close to celebrities by being privy to "inside information" about the private lives of public figures. Targets of tabloid gossip become familiar friends; indeed, more may be learned about them than is known about the real people next door or down the block. Readers may feel that they are part of an "invisible neighborhood" where, through the medium of the tabloid, they share personal information with millions of unknown but fellow gossipers across the country. This is no small benefit to those who share membership in our impersonal, rootless society—a society in which social interaction is fast becoming a rare commodity.

Although gossip columns, tabloids, and magazines have consistently published a number of positive stories, these articles have changed over the years. Before the 1960s, gossip columnists reported short, descriptive accounts, usually of the work roles of celebrities and not their private lives. In the mid-1950s, it was Robert Young working on a television pilot film; Joey Bishop emceeing a TV awards program; Jacqueline Susann at work on a novella. These columns reported new or currently held positions, work activities, and information about income or salary, as well as firings, retirements, and terminated engagements—what James Brady calls "power gossip."

Even the legendary giants of gossip—Parsons and Hopper— frequently printed news about the professional role of Hollywood celebrities. They revealed who was being cast in what films and which motion pictures were being planned. The following lead story from a Louella Parsons column published in 1960 is rather typical: "I cornered Ross Hunter at a recent party, and was happy to hear him say that when he produces Back Street, he'll make it in its entirety in the U.S.A. . . . Ross wants Efrem Zimbalist for the male lead, and he's hoping Jack Warner will give his consent because, Ross said, U-I loaned Warner's Sandra Dee for the highly successful Summer Place. Ross hopes to start Back Street in July."[12]

Beginning in the mid-1970s and continuing into the 1980s, however, the character of syndicated gossip columns has changed dramatically. The majority now focuses not on what celebrities do on the job but on their private lives—their relationships with children or spouse, their daily habits at home, or their love affairs. Moreover, only 8 percent of the gossip columns now employ dot items. Instead, the columns are dominated by gossip presented in a section or in a question–answer format. Gossip tends now to be not descriptive, but evaluative or judgmental; not simple, but complex.

The targets of gossip have also changed. There has been a general bias toward concentrating on groups whose members hold power, wealth, and prestige, while downplaying the accomplishments of women, minorities, and the poor. Targets tend to be white males—and sometimes females—who are widely recognized as "star" or celebrity people from show business: famous and successful actors, nightclub performers, dancers, television and film personalities, singers, songwriters, and the like. The names are familiar to large and diverse audiences: from the 1950s and 1960s, Redd Foxx, Carol Channing, Glenn Ford, Andy Williams, Robert Young, and Jacqueline Susann; from the 1970s and 1980s, Michael Jackson, Bruce Springsteen, and Christie Brinkley.

Despite their overall dominance, however, the representation of show people in gossip columns has declined over the last few decades. In their place, we have seen a growing presence of politicians—holders of political office, candidates, or individuals well known for their political views, people like Ronald Reagan, Jimmy Carter, Tip O'Neill, and Bill Bradley.

There has also been an increase of printed gossip about the spouses, relatives, or friends of well-known people in show business or politics. For example, when Jimmy Carter was president, people gossiped about his brother

Billy, his sister Ruth, his mother Lillian, his daughter Amy, and even about his daughter Amy's baby-sitter. We have become so hungry for celebrity gossip that even those who have merely touched the lives of a well-known politician or a Hollywood star themselves come to assume the status of celebrities about whom people will gossip.

Gossip columns have changed since the 1950s, when television was still in its infancy. They now focus less on show people and more on politicians, less on occupational gossip and more on private affairs. Most important, gossip columns have become increasingly concerned with sanctioning appropriate or exemplary behavior. Despite these changes, however, there have been constants as well. Throughout their history, syndicated columnists have been preoccupied with celebrities who are white, male, and in show business. And from the beginning, a sizable amount of printed gossip has provided public recognition for socially acceptable behavior—behavior which conforms to the small rules of our society.

The supermarket tabloids have also changed over the past few decades. To expand its middle-class market and attract respectable national advertisers, the *National Enquirer* has significantly modified both its format and its content. The gore of yesteryear is all but gone, having been replaced by stories with a positive message. The *Star* now has a number of upbeat articles and a stapled cover that looks more like that of a magazine than a tabloid. The "softening" of tabloid journalism has resulted in a previously unknown diversity of both method and content. For example, the lesser-known *Sun* still features stereotypical tabloid stories, such as "Woman Gives Birth to Black Sheep," while the *Globe* headlines "Moonlighting Star Caught Streaking." Moreover, whereas most other tabloids have a full-time staff of reporters, the *Weekly World*

*News* gets its stories by locating and rewriting weird and bizarre articles previously printed elsewhere.

———— • ————

To understand what life is like in other cultures, anthropologists often live for years among the natives they study, adopting their dress, eating habits, and living accommodations, as well as studying their language and way of life. It would not be much of an exaggeration to suggest that the gossip reporter's repertoire of techniques for collecting information is like that of the anthropologist who studies the natives in a primitive tribe or community. The anthropologist often relies on informants, "goes native" by joining in the life of a community, and gathers cultural artifacts. So does the gossip reporter.

Unlike anthropologists, however, gossip reporters are often supplied material without requesting it. For years, Hollywood agents fed columnists and reporters information, even dirt, about their clients in order to get free publicity. Legendary gossip columnist Walter Winchell was swamped everyday with gossip from agents for plugs in his widely read column. Publicists galore would scurry about collecting tidbits of news, jokes, and assorted trivia— anything that might end up in Winchell's column.

Some agents were so desperate to get a plug for their celebrities that plaintive notes were attached: "Dear Walter: Would you please use the indicated note. I need a plug. Could use some cheer these bleak days. Wife and kid hospitalized." Winchell often succumbed to such pleading notes when they were from steady contributors.[13]

During the days when Parsons, Hopper, and Graham monopolized the market for Hollywood gossip, press agents routinely offered more than just "hot tips" in return for publicity. During the 1950s, the Hollywood press could, at the very least, expect to be wined and dined by well-heeled filmmakers. Some even made it onto the regular payrolls of Hollywood publicists in return for "services rendered in print." Many reporters received free press trips or junkets, which included first-class hotel accommodations, lavish meals in expensive restaurants, and round-trip transportation. According to Hollywood writer Ezra Goodman, one veteran columnist had his entire home furnished by press agents and film producers. They supplied him with everything from washing machine and refrigerator to television set and grand piano.[14]

This still happens today, although at a level that demonstrates the reduced power of the gossip columnist to influence the behavior of the masses. At the lower end of the scale, for instance, Boston columnist Norma Nathan recently received visitors from the newly opened Lafayette Hotel, Boston. In keeping with the Swiss ownership, the women—Carolyn Morrissey and Kathy Smith—were dressed as though they were on their way to an Alpine picnic. For a possible plug in the newspaper, Nathan was given a "tribute" consisting of a basket of fruit, pastries, and Swiss chocolate.

At the upper end of the scale, syndicated columnist Aileen Mehle, better known simply as Suzy, frequently receives gifts of such items as champagne and caviar. Once, a woman whose name Suzy had mentioned in her column sent her a check for one thousand dollars. Unlike the smaller presents she accepts, however, Suzy mailed back the check along with a note saying, "You're a darling, but I don't do this sort of thing."[15]

This is not to say that Aileen Mehle's position as a major columnist has not brought her personal power and gain; it's just that she won't take a bribe. Suzy was the only woman to make *New York Magazine*'s feature story listing the ten most powerful men in New York. In 1972, the late Charles Revson nominated her to serve on the board of directors of Revlon cosmetics.

Some stars regularly use papers like the *Enquirer* to make sure that millions of readers know who they are and care about what they do. Press agents often send items of gossip with their clients' permission to reporters and columnists around the country in the hope of attracting publicity. Some publicists may make a deal with a tabloid or magazine to feature a relatively obscure client along with a more popular one. According to Richard Taylor, who is a celebrity reporter for the *National Enquirer*, "If a publicity agent can deliver us Joan Collins for an interview story, we might take a lesser actor for a little story. The reporter can't decide this independently, but he can deliver the package to the publisher. It is plausible, but it doesn't happen often."

In some cases, celebrities act as their own publicists. For example, they might phone a particular columnist in the hope of getting an item into the papers or of ensuring that their viewpoint will be represented in an item about to break. Both Louella Parsons and Hedda Hopper claimed that Hollywood celebrities often telephoned them or dropped in at their homes in order to share an "exclusive" about their personal lives. In the early days of Hollywood, when Parsons was the undisputed champion of gossip, it was regarded as "standard procedure" for a celebrity to phone her before getting married or divorced. Legend has it that one Hollywood couple postponed their elopement because they had forgotten Parson's phone number.[16]

A celebrity who "plants" an item of gossip about himself or herself with a columnist can to some degree control what will be printed and even when it will appear in print. Take, for example, a well-known couple who wish to maintain their privacy and conceal their coming wedding from public scrutiny. They could decide to "stonewall" and risk having gossip reporters secure the details of the event through their sources. Or they could make phone calls to local columnists to give the details of the wedding and ask them not to print it until a certain date. The columnists might make a deal, if they like the couple, and especially if they are convinced of eventually having a scoop.

It is important for a celebrity to get publicity at the appropriate time. The value for Dolly Parton of appearing on the cover of *People* is particularly great when she is plugging an album or a new movie. But gossip magazines and tabloids also have a timetable, and it may not coincide with that of the celebrities they wish to feature. A celebrity without a vehicle to promote may suddenly become inaccessible. *People*'s Wingo provides an example: "You couldn't get Barbra Streisand to answer the telephone now, but when *Yentl* was sinking, you had her direct number."

For decades, press agents have been sending items of gossip about their celebrity clients to reporters and columnists in the hope of attracting publicity. Anyone who looks closely at columns around the country will occasionally happen upon the same item of gossip about a particular celebrity in several different newspapers. Even the wording of the item may be identical or almost identical, indicating that its source may have been a single press agent.

Louella Parsons often used the words of a press agent, but only when she was convinced that she was the first to know. She was extremely intolerant of publicists who "double-planted" stories about their clients, that is, who gave the same story to two or more columnists while telling each of them that "that is an exclusive."[17]

Obviously, some columnists and reporters do, in fact, use items from publicists, at least occasionally. Even legendary columnist Dorothy Kilgallen did. But she would strike a bargain: For every item she ran about a publicist's client, he or she would have to submit three more items about somebody else. In effect, Kilgallen had press agents writing her column for her.

Other gossip reporters, like Boston's Norma Nathan, refuse to print items from publicists. "I send them packing," she explains. "I tell them I don't want something you're going to put in other places. I don't want junk!"

The so-called junk that finds its way into newspapers across the country certainly has a following. Wire services routinely distribute gossip, much of which is compiled and edited at the local level for "People and Places" columns. Some of these columns do not have bylines; nor do they always contain the flamboyant or exaggerated style of a full-fledged gossipist. But essentially, they contain the same sorts of gossip, even if it lacks the flair.

The *Boston Globe*'s daily "Names and Faces" column, for example, prints a mix of information about celebrities and ordinary individuals, all of which is compiled from wire reports and is not given a byline. In a recent issue, the column had items about a disk jockey in Austin, Texas, who, while doing his own program, called a competitive radio station and won a car; about jazz singer Ella

Fitzgerald's recuperation from open heart surgery; about Frank Sinatra's plan to give away tickets to his show in Madrid; about Aretha Franklin's being the first woman chosen for induction into the Rock 'n' Roll Hall of Fame; about Gloria Steinem's new talk show; about a man from Warwick, Rhode Island, who finally paid a hospital bill in the amount of $4 that he had received in 1948; and about Neil Edwards of Totnes, England, who had inherited six thousand golf balls from his grandfather.

By contrast, the *San Francisco Chronicle*'s "Personals" column bears the byline of Leah Garchik, who gives her items the appearance of full-fledged gossip by the clever use of subtitles such as "Pillars of the Community," "Who Said What," "International Incidents," and "Meow." Wire reports in Garchik's column include items about Princess Isabelle d'Orléans, who, after fifty-five years of marriage, filed for divorce from the Count of Paris; about two youths who apologized to Queen Elizabeth after trying to spray her with a water hose; about a woman who was named "Miss Man Made 1986"; and about former Senator George McGovern who was not chosen president of St. John's College.

For certain kinds of information, it may not be necessary to go directly to a celebrity, her or his press agent, or an informant. Instead, a gossip reporter may have access to public or private records (archival data in either computerized or conventional form) containing biographical statistics or life events. Background information for James Brady's weekly column in *Parade* is retrieved from a computerized data bank in which celebrity "vital statistics" are stored. We learn, for example, that Ann Margret, who was recently profiled by Brady, was born April 28, 1941, in Valsjobyn, Sweden, came to the United States in 1946, and was raised in Illinois. Her given name is Ann-Margret Olsson. She is 5 feet 3½ inches tall, weighs 110 pounds, and has green eyes and naturally brunette hair. Ann Margret married Roger Smith in 1967. She got her start in show business at the age of sixteen, when she performed on Ted Mack's "Original Amateur Hour."

Public records collected by courts and registries may be an important source of information for gossip reporters about marriages, births, deaths, divorces, and the like. Boston columnist Norma Nathan recently ran an item in her column about a local resident who purchased a car condo—a place to garage his automobile—costing $75,000. She recalls, "I called the registry of deeds and checked on it. I had to find out if the guy had a Jaguar or a Mercedes."

Even without the help of publicists, gossip reporters who usually print firsthand accounts also sometimes "borrow" items from each other, from news stories in other newspapers and magazines, or from wire service reports. Although Norma Nathan opposes publishing items planted by celebrity press agents, she herself admits both giving and taking items of gossip from other printed sources. For example, Nathan recently ran a humorous item that she got out of the *Washingtonian* magazine about Senators Kennedy and Dodd going to a Washington restaurant, where they pulled pictures of fellow Senators from the walls and smashed them on the floor. Apparently, both Senators had been drinking. According to Nathan, after she printed the story in her own column, columnist Irv Kupcinet picked it up in Chicago. Then, three weeks later, the same story came across the wire. One of the city editors at the *Boston Herald* put it on Nathan's desk and said, "Why don't we have good items like this?" It was a joke, however—he knew the source of the story.

Another example of "borrowing" between columns involves Nathan's printing an item concerning a Harvard professor who had been present during negotiating sessions between Russians and Americans. As printed, the story read that, throughout the negotiations, the Russians kept calling for tea and the Americans kept calling for water. Finally, they found themselves making more trips to the bathroom than to the negotiating table. Three or four months after it ran, an editor at the *Boston Herald* discovered the same story in Herb Caen's column in the *San Francisco Chronicle*. According to Nathan, "Either he read my column or it went on the wires."

James Brady similarly admits borrowing on occasion from magazine articles in which celebrities are featured. He is also quick to point out the importance of a columnist's giving credit in print to his published sources. He does not "steal" material from other writers, but he is also not reluctant to borrow it when he indicates its source. For example, Brady recently wrote a piece about George Bush from information he had read in a cover story appearing in the *New York Times Sunday Magazine*. In the midst of an otherwise serious *Times* interview, Brady discovered a long passage in which the vice-president defended himself for wearing button-down shirts and Brooks Brothers clothing. Brady got an entire column out of this passage.

Just as anthropologists "go native" by immersing themselves in the culture they are studying, so gossip reporters often hang around their celebrity subjects by attending their parties and social gatherings. Publicists often invite reporters and columnists to attend a party in the hope they will write about it or promote somebody in attendance. Gossip reporters become, in effect, what anthropologists call "marginal natives."

*People* magazine even has a reporter who specializes in just going to parties "full of people that you and I would recognize." Hal Wingo says that *People* constantly hears about parties from publicists, "99 percent of which are not great." Although *People* reporters are sometimes invited, they often have to crash a party by "badgering" the people promoting the party (fundraisers). If they get in, the reporters' goal is to "chronicle" everything from the dress and style of the individuals to the mood of the event. Even if they do not gain access, all is not lost. An enterprising reporter, claims *People*'s Wingo, can interview those who deliver things like flowers and food to the party.

According to longtime Washington columnist Diana McLellan, food and gossip are inseparable in the nation's capital. She calls a Washington dinner party a "covered-dish supper of gossip" and indicates that journalists are popular dinner guests. In fact, the most powerful gossip columnists are invited to dinner parties at the top level.[18]

Columnist James Brady attends parties to gather information about celebrities. But like many of his colleagues, he is also fascinated by the splendor of the wealth and success he finds at such gatherings. "There is a lot in me of the little boy outside the party with his nose pressed up against the glass," he explains. "I love to see the money and the power and the glamour—it's all in there. The difference is I now get in under the tent occasionally."

It is not difficult to understand Brady's fascination with extravagance. Indeed, in this respect, he is very much like his readers, except that he actually gets to participate in it. Take, for example, a party to which Brady was invited. It was a black tie affair that billionaire Malcolm Forbes gave on the occasion of the final voyage of his old yacht. The guest list was rich with celebrities. Even Princess Margaret attended. "You can't go to something like that," says Brady, "without coming out with at least an item and maybe a whole full-blown column."

Brady's popularity with New Yorkers ensures that he will now "get in under the tent" more than he wants to. In order to have some time to himself for writing, Brady actually must turn down certain invitations. He decided to attend a party at Bloomingdale's for the author of a book about the Harvard class of 1949 but declined an invitation to attend a party on the same evening given by the Long Island newspaper *Newsday*.

Brady might be selective in accepting invitations to parties, but he recognizes the importance of "mingling with the natives." Dinner at Elaine's restaurant provides a tremendous wealth of gossip. On any given evening, he might be seated across from the former head of Viking Press or next to a Hollywood actor. He might hear stories about Warren Beatty or Dustin Hoffman, about a soon-to-be released motion picture, or about relations between actors on the set. Brady just jots it all down, takes a few notes on a matchbox, and puts it in his pocket—until he has a chance to transform it into an item for *Advertising Age* or *Parade* magazine.

Although tabloid reporters are invited to parties, they "aren't on any A list, that's for sure," says a staff reporter for the *Enquirer*. Part of the reason is that tabloids have less prestige value than a gossip column in a daily newspaper. Celebrities often reason, says Richard Taylor, "It would be nice to have our name in Liz Smith's column, but the *Enquirer*? Well, I don't know."

Tabloid reporters get fewer invitations to parties for another reason as well: They have less control than does a regular columnist over who does and does not get into print. For example, there are at least ten celebrity reporters at the *Enquirer*. As a result, any one of them has relatively little decision-making power. But in a column, you know there's an outlet because you know you are talking to the "boss."

Columnist Janet Charlton is right in the middle: she writes a weekly column for a popular tabloid. And Charlton doesn't go to parties to have a good time; she goes to work, to pick up information and informants. Just as any other guest might, Charlton introduces herself around and chitchats with new acquaintances. But unlike those guests who attend to have a good time, she is extremely sensitive to conversations behind her and on both sides. According to Charlton, "When I hear something that I want to write down but not in front of anybody, I excuse myself to the lady's room and write it down before I forget. I train my sources to do that too."

Unlike Janet Charlton, many columnists do not attempt to hide their intentions from public view. Some go to parties with both notebook and tape recorder in hand. This open style has the advantage of maximizing the information they are able to collect; it also runs the risk of intimidating the other guests. For a columnist, this is a small price to pay, especially at large, noisy dinner parties where it is difficult to hear and guests are reluctant to talk candidly.

Of course, gossip reporters like best of all to get direct interviews with celebrities. Indeed, at times, both the anthropologist and the gossip reporter can get their data easily by going directly to the people they want to understand. Some natives are cooperative and willing to talk candidly; so are some celebrities.

At one extreme is *People* magazine, where most of the data used in the stories come from up-front interviews. With very rare exceptions, the "subjects" *People* profiles cooperate with its reporters. In fact, celebrities frequently seek out the magazine as a way to publicize a new movie, play, or record.

One of the "cardinal rules" of *People*, according to its assistant managing editor Hal Wingo, is that reporters should do stories only when celebrities allow them into their homes to observe how they behave with their spouses and children. The reasoning is that this is the most efficient strategy for understanding what people are really like in a brief period of time—short of living with them. Therefore, contends Wingo, "we don't do interviews on the road; we don't do interviews in hotels; we don't do interviews with people who don't let us get that close to them."

Despite their reputation for printing "dirt," even the supermarket tabloids, such as the *National Enquirer*, the *Star*, the *Globe*, and the *National Examiner* often are able to secure the cooperation of celebrities. In fact, as many as 40 percent of the celebrity stories in the *National Enquirer* are "up front, sit-down" interviews conducted in cooperation with the stars and their press agents. For example, the *Enquirer* recently ran an interview with William Sanderson, an actor who stars on "Newhart," where he plays sort of a dolt. The *Enquirer* story emphasized that, in real life, he is actually a bright law school graduate. The irony of the contrast between role and person, character and actor, was dramatic; it did not require the help of informants to probe beneath the surface and uncover any "dirt."

Yet the stigma of tabloids often makes it difficult for reporters to gain access to the lives of celebrities. Traditionally, anthropologists as a group have not been stigmatized; although direct contact with natives has sometimes been difficult, it is usually possible. Increasingly, however, Third World nations are rejecting the requests of anthropologists to enter their villages and study their people because of dissatisfaction with prior anthropological studies.

Tabloid reporters are also very much aware of the stigma associated with their job. At one level, it is regarded in some circles as a mark of inferior journalism and unethical practices, as a job that attracts those who are motivated not by higher principle but solely by monetary gain. Celebrity tabloid reporters must also deal psychologically with the fact that they cover the Hollywood beat, a job that, to some people, is without serious purpose or practical significance. Among journalists, tabloid gossip reporters occupy a marginal status.

Especially among Hollywood celebrities, reporters for the *National Enquirer*, the *Star*, and other supermarket tabloids must constantly live down their reputations. Tabloids may especially be avoided by stars who have highly critical opinions of papers like the *National Enquirer* and their staff. One celebrity says of these reporters, "The public never encounters the very sleazy, ratty people that work for it [the tabloid]. They are a kind of human vermin crawling around like roaches. They're nocturnal. Put the lights on and they all run for holes." Though the content of a particular story might not offend a star, the reputation of the tabloid does. According to Sam Rubin of the *National Enquirer*, "I'll call someone up and they'll yell at me, 'I'm not going to talk to you guys . . . I'm not going to talk to that paper.' "[19]

During their heyday, the reputation of certain syndicated columnists for snooping into personal affairs was not unlike that of the tabloids today. The reputation of Walter Winchell for spreading "dirt" led the *New York World* to warn its staff members to tell Winchell nothing, and in 1931, *Time* magazine wrote, "Alert, the Winchell ear hears all. Amiable, the Winchell disposition makes friends easily, elicits scandal scraps. Then, at three or four in the morning, he goes back to his typewriter and two-fingers what he has learned, adding here and there the result of an imaginative mind."[20]

Even today, gossip columnists are often seen (and feared) as being almost omniscient—privy to secrets that few people share, and that many celebrities claim they do not want shared. Tabloid reporters, even more, are seen as snooping for such secrets and as stretching the truth and standards of decency to get their stories.

Compared with their counterparts who have gossip columns in "more respectable" gossip magazines and newspapers, tabloid reporters are less likely to get invited to parties, are more apt to be ignored by Hollywood publicists, and are less well received by some segments of the general public. As one tabloid reporter put it, "In and around Hollywood, people often are astonished when they meet me. They say, 'You seem so clean cut; you seem so nice. I expected you'd be wearing a trenchcoat and dark glasses.' "

The reaction to tabloid reporters seems to be considerably more favorable in "middle America," among the very people who buy and read supermarket tabloids on a regular basis and aren't embarrassed to admit it. These are the Americans who live some distance from major metropolitan centers, but they are also the people who make up the "silent majority." As suggested by *Enquirer* editor-in-chief Iain Calder, "We are writing for Mrs. Smith in Kansas City, but she could be in Queens, New York or a suburb of Chicago. Mrs. Smith is middle America."

According to Richard Taylor, *Enquirer* reporters are regarded by middle Americans in an extremely positive light: "In Wichita Falls or Des Moines, if you're an *Enquirer* reporter, you're a hero, a star. You're fresh, exciting, different. They want to know gossip; they want to know what's happening in Hollywood. 'Wow, you live in Hollywood? Beverly Hills?' "

The situation is different in Hollywood, where tabloid reporters face a practical problem as a result of the stigma: in order to get a story, they must sell themselves to suspicious and ungrateful celebrities and their publicists. As they see it, one of the most important skills required of tabloid reporters is their ability to sell themselves. As one *Enquirer* reporter put it,

> Every day, we're calling up press people trying to get them to cooperate or give us a quote. And we're salesmen—not selling wares, but words. It is frustrating to a degree. I'm doing them a favor; but I have to hassle with them to get their second-tier TV star in a quote about his Easter wish. Eighty percent are exactly of that variety; we have a lot of trouble. If the very same story appeared in the *LA Times*, they'd be taking me out to dinner to get it in. Because it's in the *Enquirer*, they don't want it. Or, they don't know whether they want it or not. Some publicists won't deal with us at all—they have a policy not to cooperate with the *National Enquirer*.

In order to gain access to groups of people, anthropologists similarly must convince their subjects that no harm will result from the research. Whether Hollywood celebrity or Trobriand Islander, "natives" are almost always suspicious about what the outsiders are really after and how they will use the information they are given.

One tactic used by some tabloid reporters is to prove themselves by writing a flattering story about a celebrity whose press agent refuses to cooperate. Richard Taylor provides a typical example:

> I did an investigative piece on Richard Pryor about his wonderful generosity. It was a positive story—he gives a lot of his money to Black charities, to charities around the world. Then, I sent the story to his publicist in the hope that he might now deal with me.

Tabloid reporters react angrily to the aversion of some publicists to have their clients appear in supermarket periodicals. Janet Charlton, for example, argues that such publicists are really not doing their job correctly:

> The publicists who don't want their clients in a tabloid are very dumb. They are not dealing with the press intelligently. I have 20 million readers on a good week. For someone to say, "No, you can't cover this event," or "We will invite Movie Review Magazine that has 800 readers but not you," doesn't make sense. You'll find that a whole lot of journalists will not have respect for publicists for that reason—most of them don't deal with the press intelligently. They don't get what they want because they don't cooperate at all. They are very negative. They assume you're going to write something negative. But they protect their clients unnecessarily. Most publicists kiss the ground that *People* magazine walks on. But there is very little difference between *People*, the *Star*, and the *Enquirer*.

Some celebrities do not like tabloids prying into their private lives, so they and their public relations people refuse to talk with reporters. Actor James Garner, for instance, refuses to cooperate with the *National Enquirer*.

He angrily charges, "Who's going to give the *Enquirer* an interview? Nobody. They've got to make it up from other interviews. I don't read the trash. So I just don't give them the time of day. They don't exist as far as I am concerned."[21] Tabloids are left with a choice: either to go out of business as a medium of celebrity gossip, to severely limit their celebrity pieces, or to use a clandestine approach, sometimes referred to as guerrilla journalism, for the purpose of gathering information.

Reporters Richard Taylor and Sam Rubin ought to know. They cover the Hollywood beat for the *National Enquirer*, and according to Taylor, their job is sometimes made extremely difficult by a star's lack of cooperation:

> A perfect example would be a romance. We understand that XYZ's TV star is dating XYZ's producer. We contact the PR people and they don't want to talk about it. They have their own reasons. That's not going to stop us from getting the story, if she's a big enough star and it's a good enough story. At this point, we'll launch an investigation by getting to people close to them who will talk about it. This requires not only reporting skills but also playing a clandestine game.

Many stars object to what they regard as an intrusion into their personal lives by tabloid reporters. "Nobody I suppose likes to read about their marriage breaking up in print," sympathizes *Enquirer* Senior Editor Dan Schwartz. But Schwartz and others in the gossip profession justify their snooping: "They are celebrities, and they are public figures, and they live by the fact that they are celebrities, so we print it."[22]

Even some celebrities agree that losing privacy goes with the territory. Actress Lynn Redgrave, for instance, says that reporters should not "pry desperately into people's lives, but a great many people default their private lives, and if they do, then I guess they're fair game." Suzanne Somers concurs but is also concerned with the accuracy of what is divulged: "There is no privacy, but you do have a right to tell the truth. And if they're going to talk about you, they owe it to you to say it accurately and not make you out to be something you're not."[23]

Some gossip reporters are absolutely convinced that most celebrities, whether or not they admit it, are actually thrilled with the publicity they receive. In fact, their extraordinary unwillingness to talk to the press and apparent efforts to obtain privacy may be regarded by professional gossips as a disguised attempt to gain just the opposite: the attention of the public. Therefore, the more a celebrity protests, the more he or she may be regarded as inviting publicity.

Carrying their rationalization to an extreme, some reporters contend that the celebrities who protest the most are sometimes the very ones who get the biggest kick out of all the publicity. Ryan O'Neal is an appropriate example, according to Charlton. He makes a terrible fuss when someone tries to photograph him. But when people ignore him, he gets just as upset. He says, "Hey, I'm over here."

*People*'s Hal Wingo similarly contends that some celebrities have a "love–hate relationship with publicity." Referring to Jacqueline Kennedy's well-known elusiveness, he argues that it actually adds to the aura of mystery about her. "She [Kennedy] constantly complains about being bothered," observes Wingo. "And yet somehow the word always gets out that she's going to be at a certain kind of place. I think a lot of them really like the attention."

Regional columnists similarly challenge the sincerity, if not the rights, of celebrities who attempt to protect their private lives from public view. The *Boston Herald*'s Norma Nathan recalls an item about Robert Redford that appeared in her column during one of his visits to Boston. She discovered that Redford was staying at the Ritz Carlton under the name of R. Miller and invited her readers to call him there. Not surprisingly, Nathan received a letter from the actor complaining that he had received numerous phone calls before 6:30 A.M. and accusing her of "shabby journalism."

Clearly, some celebrities may be unwilling to pay the price of their stardom. They don't want to be ordinary people, but they also come out constantly against the press, even though it has essentially played a role in making them successful. Nathan cites, as a prime example, Johnny Carson's threat to sue the *National Enquirer* for $40 million. "People can't even remember the item about him," she exclaims. "It's popcorn—it's banal—but they're more banal by taking it seriously."

But, whether or not such protestations are always genuine, gossip reporters are provided with a convenient rationalization for their intrusions into the private lives of celebrities. A Hollywood star who asks to be publicized is obviously seeking publicity, but from the point of view of a gossip reporter, so too is a Hollywood star who attempts to conceal her or his private life from public view. The former is being up front; the latter, hypocritical or insincere. For a celebrity, this is a catch-22: Yes means yes and no means yes.

Anthropologists, too, rationalize their intrusions into the lives of people in other cultures. Citing the "benefits" of their research and the "pursuit of knowledge," anthropologists can justify what in everyday life would be considered impolite, rude, invasive, or snooping. Somewhat akin to the rationalization of gossip reporters, anthropologists have also justified their research by claiming that certain groups and cultures, especially those that are endangered, threatened, or just misunderstood, need to be studied so that someone can speak on their behalf.

The Madonna–Sean Penn wedding was regarded by tabloid reporters as an example of stars who are "so decidedly uncooperative, so unnecessarily secretive," that they invite publicity. According to Richard Taylor, "You cannot think for a second that that was not by design. . . . The Madonna wedding was engineered." At the *National Enquirer*, the attitude was "If they are going to try to keep it a secret, then we are really going to find out."

Were the very "hot" Madonna and Sean Penn actually attempting, as a tease, to gain the attention of the world? Whether or not they were, that is precisely what they accomplished. During the summer of 1985, reporters from tabloids, columns, newspapers, and magazines around the nation tried to cover the ceremony on a thousand different fronts. There was a general media blitz!

Three teams of *Enquirer* reporters made a concerted effort to try to cover every possible aspect of the ceremony. In the words of Sam Rubin, they did everything "to cover every possible detail, to try to penetrate security."

It was general knowledge that the wedding was to be held in Malibu, but where and when? To find out, one *Enquirer* reporter started with the bride's garbage:

> We found the guest list by rummaging through the trash. We then called one of the guests from back-east. We just said, "Hello. We'll pick you up in

a limosine when you get to L.A. When you get here, you'd better call and tell us so we can plan on how long it will take us to get you to the wedding." And we really didn't say anything else.

At this point, nobody knew where the wedding was being held, not even the guests. But the afternoon before the wedding, the guests were informed. Ours called me up and told me where the wedding was going to be. We drove where he indicated and there it was: the wedding was being held in the backyard of a large house in Malibu, right next door to Johnny Carson.

At that point, I think we were the only people to know where the wedding was located. But that advantage dissolved the next day when a wire service sent a helicopter buzzing Malibu to find out where they were setting up a tent. They put it on the wire immediately; and, in a matter of hours, everybody was there.

Every major newspaper and television station used helicopters to get pictures. It was like something right out of *Apocalypse Now*—eight helicopters buzzing around the house and some forty reporters out in front of the gates. The sound was so deafening it resembled a battlefield. We drove the guy to the wedding. We had him completely locked up. After the party, we put him back in the limo and drove him back. He gave us every detail of the wedding. He was tricked. We just said, "The limo is for the wedding." He saw it as special treatment from the bride and groom.

The Madonna–Sean Penn wedding was also a "nightmare" for *People* to cover. They didn't hire a helicopter; they just bought photographs from a free-lance service in Los Angeles that flew over the wedding. But they did want to send a reporter to the gates of the wedding itself. According to Wingo, the bride and groom sent a cryptically worded invitation telling guests to assemble at a certain location, from which they would then be taken to the wedding itself. Making it even more difficult for the reporter, the exact time of the ceremony was not indicated on the invitation.

How did *People* find out precisely where to send its reporter, as the wedding's place and time were a secret? According to Wingo, "We had a staff correspondent whose cousin was a make up man who had been invited to the wedding. He did not come back and say 'I'll give you the story,' but he was able to tell us at least where he was going. That's how we got close to it. But once this thing got started, there was such a trail of reporters from all around LA that everybody knew in thirty minutes after they got started."

Clearly, techniques other than standard up-front interviews seem justified to tabloid reporters. A few years ago, for example, the world press was keenly interested in a rendezvous in London between the then separated Richard Burton and Elizabeth Taylor. The *National Enquirer* had twenty reporters on the scene. An attractive female reporter was also dispatched to get the inside scoop from Burton. She stayed at his hotel, picked him up at the bar, and spent many hours with him. Burton admitted in the exclusive interview she obtained that he had made love to Taylor in London. Clearly, a standard up-front interview approach would not have yielded the same results.[24]

Anthropologists frequently use "disguised observation." They deliberately assume fake identities in order to gain access to closed settings and to obtain the cooperation of their subjects. In one case, several faculty members and graduate students actually joined a small group of people whose leader prophesied the imminent destruction of the

North American continent in a huge flood. In another case, a social scientist became a member of Alcoholics Anonymous, attending the weekly sessions and pretending to be a recovering alcoholic. In yet another case, a field-worker studied homosexual encounters in public restrooms by assuming the role of "watch queen," or lookout. After an encounter, he would follow his subjects to their cars in order to get the numbers of their license plates and locate their addresses through the police. Months later, wearing a disguise, he interviewed them in their homes, frequently in the presence of their wives and children, in order to determine more about their lifestyles.

To get the kind of "data" they want, tabloid reporters sometimes conceal their identity from celebrities. One example of such "covert" or disguised research happened when an *Enquirer* reporter was told to cover Frank Sinatra's trip to the Holy Land. According to *Enquirer* personnel, "I doubt he [Sinatra] still realizes that the young man who came up and threw his arms around him and had his picture taken with Frank on the flight was an *Enquirer* reporter. That man was with him for ten days without Frank even knowing he worked for us."[25]

Robert Wagner similarly failed to realize that, when he put his house up for sale, the first prospective buyer to inspect it was none other than a tabloid reporter. Nor did another celebrity know that he was seated next to an *Enquirer* reporter on a flight to Los Angeles, as he poured out his personal life; the reporter just sat, took mental notes, and wrote a story later. The star recalled, "I met my wife [to be] in Nashville and I was commuting on weekends to see her and we were really in love. And everytime I left to come back to L.A. it was really kind of heartbreaking. And on the plane back, a woman sat next to me and I told her my whole story—how much in love I was with this girl, and I knew this was the girl to live my life with. And it turned out the lady was from the *Enquirer*."[26]

Tabloids often buy stories from stringers, writers who work on a free-lance basis for many different publications. In one sense, these stringers have an advantage over tabloid staff reporters in terms of gaining the cooperation of a celebrity. They can truthfully deny working for a tabloid with a bad reputation. In fact, they may not honestly know for certain where or when their story will be published.

Good anthropologists are trained to look for "data" everywhere, not just in their routine observations and standard interviews. They might examine messages on bulletin boards, graffiti, or garbage. Tabloid reporters may similarly improvise other techniques not associated with mainstream journalism. In the late 1970s, for example, tabloid reporters made a habit of rummaging through the actual trash of everybody who was anybody. In one legendary case, *Enquirer* reporter Jay Gourley went through five bags of Henry Kissinger's throwaways, where he found a number of important government documents. When the *Enquirer* listed the contents of the Secretary of State's trash, there was quite a commotion. Kissinger had dumped— without shredding—several government memos that might have been of value to a potential assassin. For example, one document indicated the number and type of arms and ammunition supply in each Secret Service limousine. Another revealed the number of agents on duty day and night and listed the names of agents assigned to guard the Secretary of State. Other documents gave Kissinger's travel schedules and even referred to his Secret Service code name.

Janet Charlton's informants are well aware of the value of garbage in discovering some gossip-worthy item about a celebrity. Some actually go on "garbage runs" through Beverly Hills. They rummage through Barbra Streisand's trash, looking for clues to her personal life. Even trivial items like gum wrappers and empty bottles of soda have been regarded as valuable discoveries—at least valuable enough for the finder to give Janet a call and let her know about them.

In the past, some of the overt combat tactics of gossip tabloids have gotten out of hand with stars who did not cooperate. On occasion, reporters may have pursued their "victims" like private detectives trailing the suspects of a crime. This happened when James Garner was temporarily separated from his wife. The *Enquirer* was interested in whom he was dating, but Garner would not say anything. A reporter recalls, "James Garner is an excellent car driver and we were following him. He knew it, and it was just like a scene out of the 'Rockford Files.' He cut across a gas station. He went up a one-way street and he lost us very effectively. We don't always get our man." Garner confirms this bizarre episode: "They had people trailing me twenty-four hours a day. Of course, I knew who they were. I could lose them whenever I wanted to. They're not too bright."[27]

A reporter will occasionally resort to threatening celebrities in order to gain their cooperation. One novice tabloid reporter did exactly that in an attempt to get an interview with actor Michael Landon, but all it got him was fired. Landon tells us, "This fool writes me a letter where he just blackmails me. He says they're going to write all this trash about me unless I give them an interview, and if so, they're going to make me look like the king of the world. Well, what kind of press is that? Come on!"[28]

If getting a direct interview is not possible, the next best thing is to talk to people close to celebrities.

Anthropologists also rely heavily on the reports of informants among the natives they seek to study. Gossip reporters have their "sources" or "contacts" to provide them with
items about celebrities that would otherwise be inaccessible. This is nothing new. Indeed, Louella Parsons had
paid informants in pregnancy labs in and around Hollywood. She would have a pregnancy in her column even
before the proud parents knew about it.

Even today, much of the material gathered on
celebrities by gossip reporters is actually secondhand. If
stars will not cooperate, informants or "sources" will be
used to write "investigative pieces" about the personal
lives of Hollywood celebrities. They may be written without the knowledge of a star or the cooperation of her or
his publicist. In this case, the story could not be written
without the aid of informants.

Sam Rubin conceives of the *National Enquirer* as
"America's high school yearbook" because it reports on
the goings on in the Hollywood community as though it
were featuring a small-town high-school clique. In this
view, *Enquirer* reporters are no more or less than the guys
who write for the school paper. They announce to the
student body who does what with whom.

Rubin applies his yearbook model to illustrate the
use of informants by Hollywood reporters. He asks rhe-
torically, "How many people really know the story of your
lovelife? Only you and the person you're involved with.
How many people are in a position to talk about it—the
periphery group? In the life of an average person, I'd say
5 to 10, that's all. In a celebrity's life—since they have so
many people working for them—that number increases.
There is an interest factor as well, so these people make
it their business to know."

Celebrities who dine together in certain restaurants in Los Angeles might as well have made a phone call to a reporter. They know that they'll be photographed by the tabloids. For Rubin, it's like the couple in high school who show up at the big game on Friday night. They want the whole school to talk about them. That's why even Martin Mull refers to Hollywood as "high school with money."

Gossip reporters have a vast number and variety of informants who provide information about celebrities who might otherwise be inaccessible. If a star refuses to talk to the *Enquirer*, there are plenty of other people who will: bartenders, unhappy wives, hairdressers, secretaries—anybody who has a chance to eavesdrop on a celebrity. "The sources in Hollywood are as many as there are people," claims one insider. Indeed, the presence of contacts may actually determine the effectiveness of a reporter or columnist; better reporters have more and higher-quality sources.

*Star* columnist Janet Charlton feels that a "telephone book" is the whole answer to a successful columnist. She believes that it is not possible to become a columnist without having a lot of friends in a lot of places. First and foremost, one must establish and build contacts everywhere. "You can name a name and I know who to call to find out," says Charlton. "What happened to Victoria Principal? Hold on, I've got to call my Victoria Principal people."

Charlton's network of sources consists of "working people" rather than stars—people who work for stars, people who work around stars. Waitresses, busboys, hairdressers, makeup artists, extras, and coffee girls—these are the people who see and hear everything in the life of a celebrity and, for a price, are willing to tell it all to a gossip columnist. According to Charlton, "A star is going to tell you something nice about herself, but she won't tell you what happened on the set yesterday. My paid informants will!"

In a column such as Charlton's, many items focus on the everyday behavior of celebrities while shopping in malls, eating in restaurants, and so on. As a result, gossip columnists may depend on celebrity fans or groupies to supply them with tidbits of information about the star they admire. Charlton believes that fans are especially aware of what celebrities do on an everyday basis: "If they're in the supermarket, and Jacqueline Smith is shopping there, they'll follow her around and watch every move she makes. Then, they'll call me up. It gives them a purpose for following the stars and watching and listening and getting involved. They get a kick out of it and maybe they'll make a little money doing what they like to do anyway." At the supermarket or the dry cleaners, Charlton talks with clerks who might remember an interesting or funny episode involving a celebrity customer. To those who are receptive, she gives out her card and tells them to keep their eyes open for something interesting. "Give me a call," she urges. "You can make some money."

Even when a subject cooperates, additional information may still be collected from sources. *People*'s Hal Wingo says, "We never settle for what subjects tell us about themselves or their work or anything else." When stories are assigned to *People*'s reporters, they are reminded "to get good tertiaries—you've got to go out and get a lot of other people talking about this person." *People* prefers as its sources the celebrities' family members. If that isn't possible, its reporters try to get co-workers: fellow actors, producers, and directors when they are doing a story on the entertainment business. If the person is in government or Washington, they try to talk to other members of the Senate or House who have served on committees with this individual. When *People* decided to do a story on the Pope, it relied on "great sources in the Vatican who could tell us how, at the end of his day, he would take a private elevator, light up a cigar, pour himself a brandy, sit down, relax, and become this fascinating human being. He didn't tell us that, but we learned it."

But unlike the tabloids, *People* does not rely on a standing list of sources. As Hal Wingo notes, "There aren't people who are just 'sources.' They are only sources because they relate in some way to the subjects through friendship, work, whatever. Their job and profession are not to be a source. It just happens that the circumstances make them a source."

*People* does not, as a rule, pay for information from sources. It does, however, sometimes pay for the exclusive rights to certain stories. Baby Fae's mother, for example, received such a contract. In recent years, *People* has run into more unsolicited callers who expect to be paid because "other publications throw their money around. So they'll say 'so-and-so offered me $5000 if I would do this story.' " A few days before Bruce Springsteen's marriage, for instance, someone called *People* and offered to provide a description of the bridal dress for $100. But *People* already had this information.

*National Enquirer* reporters, on the other hand, have so many paid sources that they are known as the "investment bankers of gossip." Indeed, they are proud of the fact that they pay top dollar for interviews and information, and they do not believe that paying money for information destroys the credibility of that information, or that once a source is paid, that source becomes suspect.

The *National Enquirer* "resorts to a vast network of highly paid informers to find out who is doing what for whom in Hollywood. And the price tag for such information comes high." Dan Schwartz, a senior editor of the *National Enquirer*, says, "You can spend $20,000 on a story easily, when you take into account reporting time, travel expenses, hotel expenses. We've had reporters simply follow celebrities around for as long as a month." A substantial amount of money per story goes to paying off informants. "It's known that you get paid for the story ideas," notes the founder of the *Enquirer*. "That's probably why we get most of the stories."

Hollywood correspondent Don Monte sees money as the driving force behind informants and he believes this arrangement is perfectly legitimate: "In one word, the reason people give me items or give me tidbits of information is money. It is all on the books, straightforward above board. Nobody goes around handing people $100 bills. I have people that are real hustlers that know their business. This is their living. This is their livelihood."[29]

In fact, there are certain key individuals in Los Angeles and elsewhere who make a very good living by providing information to tabloids. For example, there is a woman in Hollywood who happens to be the live-in girlfriend of a noted film director. She informs on lots of her boyfriend's famous associates for fun and especially for money.

Many informants are motivated by money. Although it is rare that anthropological informants cooperate to get paid, other resources or commodities that may be exchanged may motivate them to provide information. Sometimes, an association with anthropologists gives natives some status among their peers. Food, clothing, hardware, and technology may also be shared with one's subjects in the field.

For money alone, informants may cooperate with a tabloid reporter. According to Richard Taylor, "It seems to be well-known around town that the *Enquirer* pays big bucks—more than the other tabloids—and 9 out of 10 informants want to know about the cash." One *Enquirer* tipster boasts, "If you hustle, you can make $1,000 a week easily, plus expenses. I never made less than $1,000 a week when I worked for them." One of Don Monte's sources earned as much as sixty or seventy thousand dollars in one year.

The use of sources is absolutely essential in the case of "plot development stories," which frequently appear in tabloids: What's going to happen on "Dallas"? Who's going to appear on "Dynasty"? The secret arrangements that make such forecasts possible are based in part on money. Taylor claims that, they also provide a good deal of free publicity: "We usually don't give away everything about future episodes of a series, but we certainly cheat it a lot. We certainly say, 'There's going to be a big wedding coming up. Here's what's going to happen inside the cover story this week on "Falcon Crest."' We buy the script from clandestine sources. The producers will deny this up and down, but I could not buy the scripts as plentifully and easily as I do without them."

Certain celebrities are fully aware of, and may even approve, the presence of informants in their everyday lives. "Take, for example, the fact that I know what Joan Collins wears to bed on her wedding night," says Rubin. "I doubt that Joan Collins doesn't know that that information gets to me. She may not call me and tell me herself, but she knows!"

Not all informants are paid large sums of money. Some tabloid reporters take a more casual approach to the payment of sources by viewing it as a gratuity. One celebrity reporter for a major tabloid put it this way: "As far as informants go, we have sources everywhere, from the periphery people who directly handle a celebrity—the guy who shines his shoes, his personal secretary, his wife, his girlfriend, his mother. The payment is sort of an optional thing. It's rare that you say, 'Come on tell me and I'll pay you.' But after the story is done, I'll often say, 'Gee, the paper's made a million dollars off your story. I'm happy to pay you, take you out for dinner.' "

Certain sources have a more sinister motive. They may want to get even—an angry ex-employee, a jealous starlet, or a jilted lover—and are motivated by a desire to seek revenge through the press. Revenge may also be a motive of the occasional publicist who is angry with a client and decides to teach him or her a lesson by phoning a gossip reporter and "telling all." Gossip reporters are only too happy to oblige.

It happens as often as a tabloid hits the newsstands. "For example, an actress who was 'passed over' was very friendly with a lot of the top stars in Hollywood. She hung out with them, despite the fact that she never made it herself. Maybe she needed the contacts. But she also harbored strong resentment. Her motivation to give dirt on the stars wasn't money. She'll take money, but that's not what she's getting—she's getting back!"

Gossip reporters get anonymous letters and phone calls all the time. Occasionally, they come from disgruntled domestic help. A tabloid reporter recently got a letter from a woman claiming to be Jacqueline Smith's maid, in which she related "the most unbelievable horror story" about her famous employer. The tabloid decided not to use the story, however, perhaps because it could not verify the details or because of the threat of a lawsuit.

Local columnists seem to depend a good deal on letters, calls, and tips coming from anonymous sources. Boston columnist Norma Nathan receives a lot of mail from unknown sources at the State House. For example, "I got a great memo here about a racist incident that I have to go after that is a Xerox of a memo from a Secretariat. It just comes in the mail."

Columnist James Brady will also use information supplied by an anonymous informant:

> For example, there is a guy at the *Wall Street Journal* who calls himself "Mole" when he gets on the phone with me. I don't know his name, but he's been calling me for years. "This is the Mole," he says. "How are you, Jim?" And, he gives me the latest inside stuff from the employees' bulletin board. He works down there and is probably active in the employees' union which is always fighting back and forth with management. The Mole loves to put a dig in there.

There are numerous local or regional gossip columnists whose newspapers lack either a budget or the ethics to pay sources. In order to stay in print, these gossip reporters need informants who can reveal the details of local events before they become public knowledge. Unlike those of their national counterparts, however, the contacts of local columnists are based more on long-standing friendships in the community than on expectation of payment.

Norma Nathan's column in the *Boston Herald* provides a good example. As the long-standing writer of "The Eye," she is very much aware of the need to scoop her competitors, that is, to find something of interest to her readers that nobody else has been able to get. According to Nathan, this means knowing a lot of people and then investigating to put things together. For example,

> I've got this very good story involving Maria Shriver who is going to be married here in April. And the reason I found this out is because I have a couple of friends who are interior decorators who called me. They stumbled across the local company that's going to do the lighting and provide the tent. So, I started pushing around a little bit and found out which church it was being held at. I called the church in which Cyndi Lauper had been married in Centerville and it wasn't that church. They said, "Oh, it's got to be this one." I called the second church. They had a really tough secretary. She wouldn't give me the date. But I know someone who's going to attend; so, I'll call them today. In the meantime, I've got a nice little nucleus of what's going to happen. I'm going to run it tomorrow morning.

Thus Nathan doesn't always sit back and wait for sources to call her. Like many of her counterparts who write regional columnists around the country, she frequently initiates a story by contacting her sources in the area. In some cases, these sources are located not only in local companies or television studios, but in local government as well. Sometimes, Nathan goes right to the top. She calls judges and secretariats, people at high levels of government service. She talks to lawyers whose penchant for gossiping is excercised directly in proportion to the amount of time they spend standing in courthouse corridors waiting for continuances. In a recent episode, Nathan received a call from the corporate city counsel of Boston informing her that seven women in the office were pregnant.

James Brady gets "tips" from some two hundred people a year, none of whom is paid more than an occasional lunch or a drink at a local tavern. Some of his informants are anonymous writers and callers; they may give him one tip a year. Others are personal friends who supply information on a continuing basis. He is well connected with the "Betsy Bloomingdale–Nancy Reagan set" because two of his close friends in California—transplanted easterners who are amused by the whole scene—get invited to all their big dinner parties. They'll call Brady the morning after a big affair and say, "Oh my God, you should have been there last night. Here's what Nancy said. Here's what Betsy said. Here's who showed up."

Like her counterparts in other parts of the country, Nathan will frequently base a gossip item on a number of different sources, including informants, public records, personal contacts with celebrities, and even the work of other columnists and reporters. *People* magazine's Hal Wingo calls it "triangulation." (So do anthropologists, who often approach their investigation of a culture in several different ways.)

Nathan relates her techniques for gathering information about Maria Shriver's wedding and validating its accuracy:

> If it's the Maria Shriver wedding, it's going to be in Hyannisport. You have to know there are two Catholic Churches there. This morning I dug up something I knew I'd seen in *Vanity Fair*, so I read it again. That gave me two words I can use in my piece—that her wedding dress is by Mark Bohan. It's going to seem very small when it comes out, because I'll have the

date, I'll have the Church, I'll have the tent, the light-
ing, plenty of stuff. But the Kennedys don't give any
information. They have a vision of themselves that is
ridiculous.

Stories are occasionally "stretched," especially if
stars will not talk to reporters and material is based only
on sources. As one gossip reporter notes:

> If a star won't talk to us about a romance, we would
> have to have at least two independent sources telling
> us about that romance, using the word "romance" or
> "love." For example, the maitre d' in a restaurant sees
> two people together—you know, a celebrity and a
> friend, and there may not be any romance. But if you
> can get enough people to say "yes, they sat in a res-
> taurant with lights in their eyes throughout the entire
> meal—they couldn't take their eyes off of each other
> or there was love in their eyes"—if you can get people
> to tell you this, then you have a romance even if the
> celebrities say there's no romance.[30]

Even a former tabloid editor was not above stretching his material. Malcolm Balfour describes how he generated predictions for the *Enquirer* when he was in charge
of this task. He and his staff of reporters began by downing
a few cases of beer. Then, they sat around and just let the
predictions flow. Finally, the psychics would go through
the list and decide which predictions they agreed with.
These were the items that got into print. According to
Balfour, "they were much more readable than the predictions the *Enquirer* psychics would make. I had some very
psychic reporters!"[31]

Since the middle 1970s, *Enquirer* editors have become
increasingly concerned about the effect of inaccurate stories

on the public image of their tabloid. To deal with the accuracy problem, *Enquirer* chairman Pope hired Ruth Annan, a sixteen-year veteran of *Time* magazine, to set up a research department in 1976, after he was embarrassed by a story that claimed Walter Cronkite believed in UFOs. At the time, Robin Leach (later of "Lifestyles of the Rich and Famous") had written the story about Cronkite, presumably based on an interview he claimed to have had with the anchorman in an elevator at the studios of CBS. After the article appeared, however, Pope received a phone call from an upset Walter Cronkite, who denied that he had ever been interviewed by Leach or that he had told anyone he believed in flying saucers. Not knowing what to believe, the surprised and embarrassed *Enquirer* executives never again asked Leach to do free-lance work for them.

Annan sees her sixteen-member department at the *Enquirer* as "the watchdog of the operation," designed to minimize the risk that another incident like that involving Cronkite could occur again. She says, "We police the copy. We verify the quotes that are in the stories, the background information. We're the reason the story is killed. We all know we're not here to run a popularity contest. We have a job to do and we do it."[32]

A critic of the research department is quick to point out that it does not know what is omitted from a story: "They do not know that you may have called 97 people who told you it's not true because all they see in front of them is a story quoting three people who tell you it is true."[33]

What critics do not say, however, is that the *Enquirer*'s research staff requires its reporters to tape-record interviews with experts and then, frequently, to check the validity of the final version of a story by reading it to the source in its entirety before publication. The research team also has the responsibility of verifying the credentials of experts who are quoted or cited in print. Precisely how much this procedure adds to the accuracy of *Enquirer* articles is difficult to estimate. What is not difficult to say, however, is that many mainstream daily newspapers do not make this a standard practice. They do not ask their reporters to use tape recorders, to verify the accuracy of quotations, or to check the veracity of credentials.

Even the validity of studies by objective and ethnical anthropologists is sometimes questioned. Clearly, anthropologists try very hard to present an accurate picture of the cultures they study. There are also a number of exceptions, however, in which anthropologists have made serious mistakes and have even harmed the people about whom they have reported.

Writing in the *New York Times*, anthropologist Richard Shweder recently argued that many classic books in his field "do not have all their facts straight."[34] Part of the problem may be that anthropologists who study a particular culture feel compelled to write an entertaining account of their experiences, so that people will read it. Anthropologists are indeed motivated to obtain the truth, but they also want status in the eyes of their colleagues and prestige in the eyes of the community. They must also be able to justify their work to government agencies, foundations, and universities by pointing to the important revelations their research has uncovered—by showing they have "scooped" their associates.

Whatever the reason, even anthropologists with the best reputations have been accused of drawing invalid conclusions. In her classic study of the Samoans, Margaret Mead concluded that the people she had studied were peaceful and happy, and that growing up sexually as an adolescent was a process free of the guilt and tension so common in American society. The basic accuracy of Mead's claims, however, have been challenged recently by fellow anthropologists as well as by the very subjects of her study. A prominent Australian anthropologist has maintained that Mead completely missed the mark. His research suggests that Samoan society contains social conflict, crime, and tension, and that coming of age there is hardly the idyllic process Mead described but is rife with turmoil.

Clearly, our purpose throughout this chapter in making comparisons with anthropologists has not been to single them out for criticism. With very similar results, we might as easily have focused our attention on the activities of psychologists, detectives, investigative reporters, or even ordinary people. Just as clearly, we do not wish to excuse or justify the behavior of gossip reporters when it is unethical or vicious. Instead, we hoped to put such behavior in perspective, so that it is neither exaggerated nor seen as peculiar to the gossip industry.

It is undoubtedly wrong when a tabloid reporter harasses or threatens an uncooperative celebrity. It is wrong when a gossip columnist knowingly prints false information. But it is just as wrong when a behavioral scientist fabricates conclusions. This is exactly what happened several years ago when British psychologist Cyril Burt, whose data "proving" that intelligence was largely inherited, turned out to have falsified his crucial evidence.

Keeping things in perspective, we again point out that many tactics and strategies are used by gossip reporters whose morality is acceptable to some but not to everyone. Is it unethical to use an informant to collect information about a celebrity? Perhaps, but police investigators do it a great deal; so do anthropologists. Is it unethical for a gossip reporter to use deception by not informing a celebrity that he or she works for a newspaper? Maybe, but psychologists routinely build deception into their experiments in order to fool their subjects; sometimes even anthropologists do it.

Despite the popular image, the behavior of gossip reporters is, on the whole, quite ethical in terms of both what they print and how they get information. Certainly, gossip columnists and tabloid reporters have no monopoly on evil or injury. As we shall see, much more dangerous gossip may exist elsewhere, but not where we expect to find it.

# Chapter 4    "ALL THE NEWS THAT'S FIT TO WHISPER"

Gossip serves to remind members of the community of the importance of its norms and values. On the negative side, gossip may be used to punish those who transgress and, at the same time, to warn everyone else not to transgress, lest they be shunned as well. Reporting the liabilities of other people through gossip issues a warning: "With every bit of gossip comes the unspoken refrain suggesting, 'So you had better do thus' or 'Beware of ever doing thus.' " In his study of a small town he called Plainville, sociologist James West similarly reported, "People report, suspect, laugh at, and condemn the peccadilloes of others, and walk and behave carefully to avoid being caught in any trifling missteps of their own."[1]

But if the behavior of an individual is approved, then gossip may instead be used to grant public recognition and to act as a reward. We already saw this in connection with gossip columns and supermarket tabloids, both of which tend to print flattering gossip about well-known people.

Similarly, everyday gossip often has a strong moral component that may be especially pronounced in small communities, where the activities of most people are highly visible to all and are easily inspected. In such cases, gossip can be a powerful mechanism of social control. It holds many people—neighbors, friends, and kin—within the cultural rules of their group.

In 1984, anthropologist Sally Merry suggested that the social control function of everyday gossip is more complex than is usually believed; in fact, it controls behavior only when those who gossip can also exercise other forms of power over its victims. For those who are economically dependent on others, this may mean loss of a promotion, a raise, or even a job. For example, individuals responsible for hiring may rely on reputations for reliability and trustworthiness to determine who will get a job and who will not. If a rumor is flying that a person has a history of unreliability, it may mean that he or she will be eliminated from the pool of candidates for a job, whether or not the gossip is accurate. In the political arena, potential candidates for office may decline to run if they know that an opponent possesses an item of gossip about them or their family that could be humiliating if made public during the course of a political campaign. Socially, the victim of gossip may be ostracized, ignored, and ridiculed. In some cultures, this reaction takes the form of nasty nicknames, mocking songs, practical jokes, nightly attacks, or insulting remarks directed against a target. The vulnerable victim who looks for a mate may no longer be permitted to marry. Or at the extreme, an individual who has been regularly accused of breaking important rules, such as those against lying or committing sorcery, may be exiled or executed by the Eskimo, the Nandi of East Africa, the Zapotec villagers of Mexico, the Navaho Indians, and some African and European societies.[2]

There are some people in every society who are more-or-less impervious to malicious gossip. A few of them are so down on their luck that they see absolutely no possibility of enhancing their reputation, no matter how exemplary their behavior. Others may be so powerful or wealthy that they actually ignore or defy gossip; their status in the community is largely immutable and therefore independent of everyday small talk.

Media gossip has similarly protected the very powerful from the scorn of public scrutiny. According to Mark C. Miller at the Johns Hopkins University, the most powerful people in the country usually don't get smeared by the press, whereas those who lack power are considered fair game. This can be seen, for example, in the allegation that many members of Congress have alcohol problems and lead deviant sex lifes, yet these allegations rarely appear in the newspapers.[3]

The ability of gossip to control behavior also depends on its social and cultural context. In simple communities, there is literally no place to hide for those who have been victimized by gossip. The values and goals they have violated are widely shared. Their entire social network—friends, relatives, and neighbors—resides in the community. As a result, the transgressor is at the mercy of fellow community members.

In modern, urban society, gossip may have lost some of its grip as an informal agent of social control. Where the informal methods break down, formal mechanisms of control are imposed, for example, law enforcement personnel, courts, prisons, and mental hospitals.

Everyday gossip is, of course, still around; but it doesn't always have the power that it possesses in small, simple societies. For one thing, our society contains numerous subgroups, based on racial, religious, and ethnic similarity, each one containing its own peculiar yet overlapping set of norms and values. What is regarded as right and proper among the members of one subgroup may be seen as wrong and improper among the members of another. What is regarded as scandalous in one place may be defined as respectable and avant-garde elsewhere.

Modern societies also provide numerous opportunities for mobility. Not only are we able to move in and out of groups in a particular community, but we can move our residence as well, sometimes thousands of miles. Rejection in one place does not necessarily mean rejection in another place. Rejection by one set of people does not always lead to rejection by others. Hence, we have a reduced vulnerability to gossip, although at a price.

For example, physicians whose reputation is questioned in one community can move their practice to another community in order to escape gossip about their professional ability. Frederick Huffnagle, an orthopedic surgeon in Massachusetts, was forced to do this when he was put on probation after scheduling experimental surgery for a patient without prior consultation.[4] Dr. Huffnagle had never performed the hip replacement technique before, and it had never been tried at his hospital. Moreover, the hospital lacked the proper equipment for this surgery.

Because of this incident and others, the executive committee of the hospital's medical staff recommended that Huffnagle's privileges not be renewed. Did this stop Dr. Huffnagle from practicing medicine? Not at all; in fact, he continued to see patients in the community. Only in the face of an increasing number of malpractice suits did he decide to leave Massachusetts. Did this stop Dr. Huffnagle from practicing medicine? Still not; instead, he moved his practice to California, where he gained staff privileges in a community hospital. On his application for a position with this hospital, he denied that his hospital privileges had ever been suspended elsewhere and that there had ever been professional liability cases against him.

Social change has also reduced the efficacy of gossip by broadening the range of behaviors regarded as socially acceptable. We are much harder to shock now. As William Buckley recently observed, "The phrase 'outrageous behavior' describes stuff that's almost hard to imagine now. I mean, Gerry Studds, the congressman who did it to the page boy, later got reelected, didn't he?"[5]

There are important exceptions in which gossip continues to have a powerful effect on social control. Negative gossip about a particular employee can reduce chances for raises and promotions; moreover, the office grapevine has been known to follow a victim from job to job. At the extreme, an individual who has served time in prison and becomes an ex-con may find himself or herself severely restricted in terms of finding decent employment. Many ex-cons have taken advantage of the fluidity of our society to move away from the community in which they had committed their crime to a city in which their former reputation is unknown. There is always the possibility of "discovery" by gossipmongers in the new community, however.

Even in modern society, there are close-knit ethnic enclaves whose members erect barriers to mobility outside the community. Under such conditions, everyday gossip continues to have a powerful influence on community members. Merry discusses the situation of Chinese residents of a small housing project located in the heart of a major eastern city. They were close-knit, dependent on one another for earning a living, and shared the same set of values. Most spoke little English; the focal point of their lives was Chinatown. This is where they worked, played, and could obtain medical, legal, and social services. Without knowledge of the English language, moving away was all but impossible.[6]

Gossip within the Chinese community was pervasive and powerful. Members would discuss "women who gamble too much and fail to take care of their families, men who have affairs and desert their wives, women who fail to repay gifts of tea cakes, and kinsmen who fail to provide assistance for weddings."[7] Only a few Chinese residents were able to ignore gossip; they were the ones who had formed social networks in the Caucasian community by dating or marrying Caucasians or by developing job skills that could be used outside.

By contrast, black residents of the same housing project as the Chinese moved easily outside their community, held diverse norms, and depended very little on one another to earn a living. For them, the costs of being the targets of malicious gossip and scandal were relatively mild. Therefore, they felt less concerned about the possibility of others' talking about them.

To emphasize this point, Merry describes the situation of a young man whose money, expensive car, and offers of jobs had made him an influential leader among his friends. When his economic status declined, however, so did his position in the group. Rather than remaining at the center of his group of friends, he was now often seen walking the project by himself.

At this point, the young man was caught slapping around his former girlfriend, who also happened to be a popular project resident. This incident touched off a wave of gossip among the residents: "He does it with little boys, right here in the playground. . . . He never went to college at all, as he claims, but dropped out of school in the eighth grade and attended one semester of special remedial college. . . . He says he is your friend but you tell him your private affairs and he tells everyone else."[8]

The young man was able to escape the potentially disastrous effects of gossip by immediately moving out of the project and moving in with friends two blocks away. He soon formed a new set of allies, including some old ones from the project, and eventually collected a new group of followers. Gossip had an impact on his life, but hardly the impact that it would have had on someone forced to remain within the boundaries of a close-knit society.

In modern societies, informal and formal mechanisms of social control often feed one another. Casual small talk about deviant activity can make its way to the formal agencies of social control. During the eighteenth century, police departments placed their spies in neighborhood cafés and meeting halls to overhear gossip and report on suspicious behavior. Germany's Nazi regime was notorious for its use of neighbors and family members as informants; much of their "evidence" about anti-Nazi activities was based entirely on unsubstantiated gossip.

In contemporary American society, official spying may not occur on a widespread basis, but nosy neighbors might inadvertently discover unlawful behavior, in the process directing the attention of law enforcement officials to illicit drugs, spouse abuse, or possession of stolen property. In court, judges may depend on gossip collected by police officers concerning the community reputation of both defendants and victims.

The mass media have given new impetus to the social control function of gossip in a complex, large-scale society. At the same time that the power of everyday gossip has waned, the influence of media gossip has grown by leaps and bounds. The key to the power of media small talk is its ubiquity: not unlike the situation in a small cohesive community, a victim once again has no place to hide. Even if he or she becomes famous "for fifteen minutes," this is long enough to ensure that the transgression will follow him or her everywhere.

Those who depend for their power on achieving and maintaining favorable public opinion—even the rich and famous—must be especially cognizant of media gossip because they are particularly vulnerable to it. Gossip definitely acts as a constraint on public people. Only the degree and circumstances of that constraint are under dispute. Entertainers depend on fan loyalty; they must be careful to watch their step and not to disappoint their admirers. Similarly, politicians need votes to be elected and/or reelected. They, too, must consider the effect of gossip on their public image. Like entertainers, they must be careful not to offend their constituents.

As we have seen, gossip columnists have frequently decided not to print an item of gossip about a particular celebrity. This may have been especially true before the Watergate era made cynics of us all. But during the 1960s, reporters still had enough respect for the Office of the President to occasionally refuse to print an item of gossip, in the interest of a greater good: to preserve the public image of our government officials. While they were in office, for example, the Kennedy brothers were treated with kid gloves. Syndicated columnist Liz Smith argues that even their involvement with Marilyn Monroe was never exploited by columnists.

There does seem, however, to be a point beyond which gossip reporters will not permit public officials to go with impunity. According to Liz Smith, Chappaquiddick changed all the Kennedys' immunity to gossip: "You couldn't find a reporter in Washington who didn't want to go for the jugular. They had all been observing Teddy Kennedy for a long time; both *Time* and *Newsweek* had reporters on that trip to Alaska in 1969 where he got drunk on the plane and misbehaved quite badly; and nobody reported it because they didn't want to hurt him. But Chappaquiddick was the end."[9]

Chappaquiddick is a tiny island off Cape Cod; it is also a code word for the tragic event in which a twenty-eight-year-old woman lost her life and a popular U.S. Senator lost his opportunity to become a candidate for the presidency.

On the night of July 18, 1969, Mary Jo Kopechne drowned when a car driven by Senator Edward (Ted) Kennedy plunged off a rickety bridge into a pond on Chappaquiddick Island. The couple had just left a party attended by five men and six single women and were riding down a lonely country road when their car veered off the bridge. More than ten hours later, Kennedy finally reported this accident to Martha's Vineyard police. And for several days afterward, he maintained a veil of silence, appearing in public only to attend Mary Jo Kopechne's funeral and otherwise retreating to the seclusion of the Kennedy family compound on the opposite side of Nantucket Sound.

A week after the fatal accident, Kennedy pleaded guilty in a crowded Edgartown, Massachusetts, courtroom to charges that he had operated "a certain motor vehicle upon a public way in said Edgartown and did go away after knowingly causing injury to Mary Jo Kopechne without stopping and making known his name, residence and the number of his motor vehicle." The plea bargain, resulting in a guilty plea, gave Kennedy a two-month suspended sentence. It also eliminated the possibility of a potentially nasty courtroom trial that might have raised some politically sensitive questions concerning his credibility, courage, and fidelity.

Like other successful candidates for public office, Kennedy understood well the necessity for anticipating and responding to the desires and anxieties of his constituency. He also understood that gossip and scandal, left unchecked and uncontrolled, might easily determine the shape of public opinion and ruin his political career. Thus, ten hours after his brief appearance in an Edgartown courthouse, Kennedy spoke on television to an estimated audience of thirty-five million Americans. He confessed to having fled in panic from his submerged automobile and Mary Jo Kopechne's body. Calling his behavior "indefensible," he asked the voters of his home state of Massachusetts to guide him in deciding whether or not to resign from the U.S. Senate.

But Kennedy also defended himself against charges of infidelity and immorality: On the evening of the Chappaquiddick episode, he had attended a cookout for "a devoted group of Kennedy campaign secretaries." He had left with Mary Jo, he claimed, for only the most innocent of reasons: to give her a lift back to the Chappaquiddick–Martha's Vineyard ferry slip (Kennedy was registered at the Shiretown Inn in Edgartown, across the channel from Chappaquiddick; Mary Jo stayed at The Dunes, a motel several miles away). Making direct reference to gossip about his relationship with Mary Jo, Kennedy was firm in his denial: "There is no truth, no truth whatever, to the widely circulated suspicions of immoral conduct that have been leveled at my behavior and hers regarding that evening. There has never been a private relationship between us of any kind."

Kennedy's nationwide television speech left serious questions unanswered and raised a few that had not been asked before. Rather than ending public speculation, it probably only helped provide the conditions of uncertainty under which scurrilous gossip tends to thrive. As political columnist Jack Anderson suggested, "If he'd just bared his soul about what happened that night, I think the press would have left him alone. But when he gives an incomplete and vague and inconsistent explanation, the press is right to look behind it."[10]

By maintaining silence and speaking only through his lawyers, Kennedy's "deliberate ambiguity" may have done little to discourage rumors. But his plea for guidance from the people of Massachusetts was more successful: it precipitated a flood of phone calls, telegrams, and letters urging him not to quit. Polling their listeners, radio stations in Boston recorded pro-Kennedy majorities ranging from

3–2 to 4–1. The major television stations in Boston each said that the sentiment of the callers was heavily supportive of Kennedy. At the state level, his future seemed secure.[11]

The national reaction was a different story: A Gallup Poll taken a month after the Chappaquiddick tragedy indicated that Ted Kennedy had suffered a major loss of popularity and confidence among Democratic voters. Perhaps they were thinking of the need for a presidential candidate to respond rationally under pressure; perhaps they were concerned with the way national leadership is expected to behave in a crisis. Whatever their rationale, only 30 percent of all Democrats questioned voiced support for Kennedy as a party leader during the next three years (this figure was down from 45 percent in a February poll). A second Gallup survey taken four months after Chappaquiddick suggested that Kennedy had not bounced back from his loss of national appeal. In November, only 28 percent of the 1,514 people sampled gave the Senator a "highly favorable" rating. The Gallup report also indicated that his losses had come equally from Protestants and Catholics, and from all age groups. Gallup asked, "Suppose you could ask Senator Edward Kennedy any question you wished to about his July 18 car accident on Chappaquiddick Island. What specific questions would you most like to ask?" Seven out of ten respondents had questions, including (in order of frequency of being mentioned): Why didn't he report the accident sooner? Why was he on that road? Why was he with the girl? Was he drinking? Why didn't he try harder to save the girl? Why wasn't his wife with him? Why was he at the party? and Was there another woman in the car?[12] In a national poll for *Time*, Louis Harris found that a majority of his respondents agreed that "there has been no adequate explanation of what he (Kennedy) was doing at the party or with the girl who was killed."[13]

Predictably, much gossip was precipitated by Kennedy's silence during the days following the death of Mary Jo Kopechne and his subsequent failure to explain or fully to disclose details of the Chappaquiddick incident (especially about the hours-long gap between Kennedy's accident and his appearance at the Edgartown police station to report his accident). All of a sudden, stories about previous Kennedy blunders and transgressions were dredged up to be told and retold, printed and reprinted, played and replayed across the nation: Ted's repeated arrests for traffic violations while a law student at Virginia, his suspension from Harvard for cheating, and a drunken airplane ride from Alaska to Washington, which had never been published before.

Much of the gossip seemed designed to explain Kennedy's behavior psychologically by confirming or reinforcing suspicions that he had a history of shallow and irresponsible behavior. There was talk about his numerous pranks, such as landing a plane without being adequately trained and riding a bucking bronco in the West. There was also talk about his indiscreet sexual behavior—the many times he had been caught flirting with pretty girls; his marital difficulties with his wife, Joan; and the time he had been seen with a lovely blond on Aristotle Onassis's yacht. The Chappaquiddick tragedy suddenly made all such gossip seem pertinent.[14]

Editorial writers around the country discussed and debated every angle of the incident. Many called for complete disclosure of the events surrounding Kennedy's accident and suggested that Kennedy's political future was being endangered by speculation and the rumors that were now being bruited about.

Like other newspapers, the *New York Times* editorialized that it was "indefensible—or so it seems in the present state of our knowledge—for the Senator to fail to seek immediate help from occupants of a nearby house, to walk more than a mile past other houses to confer with friends, to bring them back to the scene of the accident still without notifying anyone else and to delay informing the police for many hours, until the next morning." The *Times* was also highly critical of Kennedy's silence following the tragic event: the fact that he had locked himself away in the Hyannisport family compound only reinforced the suspicion that his primary motive throughout the ordeal had been to maintain his political position in the eyes of the voters. As a potential candidate for the presidency, "it is necessary carefully and objectively to examine his conduct in times of extreme stress."[15]

Hoping to define an ambiguous political situation, readers sent thousands of letters to magazines and newspapers; radio and television responded by featuring the episode whenever possible, even during prime time. Psychiatrists also got into the act by suggesting that Kennedy's accident and his behavior after it may have represented an unconscious desire to avoid the burdens of becoming a presidential candidate.[16]

A few months after the tragic episode, Jack Olsen, a senior editor for *Sports Illustrated* who had investigated the Chappaquiddick affair for a book, speculated that Kennedy was not driving the car—was not even in it—when it went off the Dyke Bridge and into the pond. According to Olsen, there was simply no way for Kennedy to have committed such an obvious blunder, whether or not he was sober. The bridge was plainly visible, and no accidents had occurred there in twenty years. Moreover, it would have required a major miracle for Kennedy to have escaped, underwater, through the window of the door on the driver's side of his car.

Olsen conjectured that Kennedy and Kopechne were headed for the bridge when they were spotted by a local policeman (actually, Deputy Sheriff Christopher Look says he saw Kennedy's black car heading for Dyke Bridge more than an hour after Kennedy testified that he had passed that way). It was after midnight, and Kennedy was concerned about the political and personal fallout of being discovered with Mary Jo, so he jumped out of the car and walked back to the party, leaving Kopechne to drive his Oldsmobile back by herself. Unfamiliar with either the car or the road, she wandered off the bridge at twenty miles an hour. Kennedy didn't learn of Mary Jo's accident until the next morning, when—for the sake of his reputation—he concocted the story about being in the car with Kopechne and making a wrong turn on his way to the ferry.

Syndicated columnist Jack Anderson reported an account of Mary Jo Kopechne's drowning that differed a great deal from both Olsen's and the Senator's. Based on information from unnamed "friends of Kennedy," Anderson charged that Kennedy and Kopechne had no intention of returning to the ferry slip but were heading for a midnight dip together. He also claimed that Kennedy never swam the channel to Edgartown, as he had testified, but instead took a row boat to the other side. Most damaging, Anderson wrote that Kennedy had begged "his cousin, Joe Gargan, to take the rap for him" by falsely admitting that he, and not Kennedy, had driven the car in which Mary Jo's body was found.

Before Chappaquiddick, relations between Anderson and Senator Kennedy had been quite cordial, if not friendly. As a result, Anderson's allegations did not appear to be malicious, even to those who questioned their accuracy.[17]

Another version of the Chappaquiddick incident explained why Rosemary Keough's handbag was found in Kennedy's car, after it was extricated from the pond. This story circulated around Washington by word of mouth and was later summarized in the August 15 issue of *Time* magazine, without a source. In this version, a federal agent had been secretly assigned to guard Kennedy. At about 11 P.M. on the night of the fatal accident, the agent observed an apparently tired Mary Jo Kopechne leave the cottage party and go to sleep in the back seat of Kennedy's Oldsmobile. Later that night, according to this story, Kennedy got into his car accompanied by Rosemary Keough, another woman at the party. Unaware that Mary Jo was asleep in back, they drove off toward the Dyke Bridge. Both Rosemary and Kennedy were able to escape from the submerged automobile, but Mary Jo drowned.

Kennedy was well aware of Chappaquiddick's political fallout, at least in the short run. Soon after his television speech, he announced that he had decided to remain in the office of Senator from Massachusetts and to seek reelection the following year. But Kennedy's position as a candidate for the presidency was another matter. He effectively deferred his candidacy until 1976 at the earliest by promising to serve the full term if reelected to the Senate. His decision was no surprise to other politicians, who understood the influence of public opinion. Senator George McGovern, for example, declared about Kennedy, "I became convinced after a fairly lengthy talk that no conceivable circumstance would bring him back into the picture. I fully expect, however, that he will be President some day."[18]

Like many others, McGovern may have underestimated the long-term impact of Chappaquiddick on Kennedy's presidential aspirations. The reasoning seemed to be that, even if gossip harms reputations, it has the life span of a housefly and will quickly be forgotten. But journalists were hardly ready to give up their quest for answers about the inconsistencies and contradictions concerning the Senator's mishap. In 1976, for example, an eight-month investigation by two Associated Press reporters produced results that resurrected doubts concerning the accuracy of Kennedy's version of the events surrounding Mary Jo's drowning. In a seven-thousand-word article, Michael Putzel and Richard Pyle reported that the Senator did not actually swim across the harbor at the time he said he did, that tidal conditions at the time of the accident were not as described by the Senator, and that the dashboard clock that Kennedy claimed he had used in order to fix the time never even existed.[19]

As the 1976 Massachusetts primary approached, Kennedy continued to be plagued by the ghost of Chappaquiddick, even in his home state. Massachusetts voters who had always supported the "Kennedy boys" voiced their skepticism about Ted's role in the fatal accident, continuing to question his suitability as a presidential candidate. The prevailing sentiment was well summarized in the statement of a middle-aged widow in Boston, who told a reporter, "He's an excellent Senator, but I don't want him for President. What will he do in a crisis? Run like he did at Chappaquiddick?"[20] In 1976, a relatively obscure peanut farmer from rural Georgia took the Democratic nomination and the presidency. Kennedy never had a chance.

Incredibly, almost nothing had changed by the 1980 election campaign. The story of Chappaquiddick was back in the news again. More important, it was back in the minds of the electorate—the campaign issue that would not go away. In a national Gallup/*Newsweek* poll, 55 percent of those interviewed said they believed Kennedy had acted improperly after his 1969 accident. Indeed, the number of Democratic and independent voters who were reluctant to rally behind Kennedy because of Chappaquiddick actually increased, despite the fact that the tragedy had happened ten years earlier. A *New York Times*/CBS poll also found shrinking support for the Senator; those questioned who disliked him as a presidential candidate repeatedly mentioned their doubts about Chappaquiddick.[21]

If anything, the gossip was thicker and more harmful in 1979 and 1980 than it had ever been. In November, CBS correspondent Roger Mudd interviewed Kennedy in a nationwide telecast that shed no new light on the Chappaquiddick incident. The Senator's apparent lack of candor in response to Mudd's questions about the events of that July evening did little to dispel the nagging doubts. Nor did it help that Jimmy Carter was believed by many reporters to have made coded references (for example, "panicked" and "steady in an emergency") to Kennedy's failure to rescue Mary Jo or to seek help.

Just before the January Democratic caucuses in Iowa, stories in the *New York Post*, the *Washington Star*, and *Reader's Digest* raised new challenges to the Senator's account of the accident and to his credibility generally. *Reader's Digest* concluded that, when his car went off the Dyke Bridge, Kennedy was driving at a much faster speed than he claimed. Both the *Washington Star* and *Reader's Digest* suggested that Kennedy's story was "false" when he claimed to have swum across Edgartown Harbor against a dangerous tide. These sources concluded instead that the tide had actually been flowing in the opposite direction and would have helped the Senator during his swim.[22] In a story that did not bear directly on the tragic accident, the *New York Post* reported that Kennedy had allegedly thrown previous parties on Martha's Vineyard for his aides and various young women.[23] The implication was clear enough.

Into the middle 1980s, Kennedy's career continued to be haunted by the ghost of Mary Jo Kopechne. In 1982, for example, the Life Amendment Political Action Committee ("Citizens Organized to Replace Kennedy") produced a pamphlet entitled "Every Family Has One" or ". . . Even a Black Sheep Can Make It . . . Especially If He's a Rich Black Sheep," which, in comic book form, dug up every item of dirt ever printed about Kennedy's past, including Chappaquiddick.[24] For example:

> Teddy cheated on a Spanish exam by getting another student to take the test in his place.
> So, Teddy decided to join the Army (ours). He signed up for 4 years. His dad had it changed to 2 years. Teddy was assigned to guard the supreme Nato headquarters in Paris. This was much more dangerous than the soft duty in Korea (This was during the Korean War) many of the other Massachusetts boys were getting.

While playing Rugby for Harvard, Teddy went kind of wild in a game. He got into 3 fist fights and had to be thrown out of the game . . . Teddy was the only player the referee had to eject in 30 years of officiating.

While at U.V.A., Teddy broke the law for the first time. . . . In all Teddy was arrested at least 4 times! Charges included reckless driving, racing with an officer to avoid arrest, operating a motor vehicle without an operator's license. His license was never revoked. Would your license have been revoked?

Then, on July 18, 1969, as America's first lunar heros were heading for the moon, another famous American was heading for a bridge. . . . The married Senator, Teddy Kennedy, attended a party with four other married men (and one single) and six single girls. While crossing Dyke bridge, Teddy drove the car off the side. A SINGLE GIRL, MARY JO KOPECHNE, WAS KILLED!

O.K.!! But Teddy said that he was dazed and left the girl in the car while he was groggy!! But he left her for OVER NINE HOURS! Just one telephone call would have summoned help, and, in the opinion of the frogman who got Mary Jo's body out, she could have been saved! Just one call! . . . Actually, 17 calls were made on Teddy's credit card BEFORE the accident was reported . . . on the 18th call . . . nine hours later . . . after she was dead. What was his sentence? Two months . . . suspended.

What can we learn from the reaction to Chappaquiddick about the effect of gossip on public opinion? (1) The impact of gossip can be long-term. The memory of American public opinion seems to have spanned Kennedy's entire career. (2) The political impact of gossip can be selective. Chappaquiddick never destroyed Kennedy's senatorial career, only his opportunity to become a viable presidential candidate. (3) Once a public figure crosses that fine line defining permissible transgressions, he or she becomes extremely vulnerable to the impact of negative gossip. (4) Gossip does indeed have a significant impact on public figures in a democratic society, even in an open, mass society. Perhaps it is true that we no longer expect perfection from our public servants, but they still must meet minimal standards. Many politicians believed that Kennedy's stand on issues would eventually overshadow Chappaquiddick. The nomination of Jimmy Carter by the Democratic Party in 1976 and 1980 put that argument to rest. At the national level, Chappaquiddick may have been Ted Kennedy's Watergate.

If gossip can have such pronounced consequences, why has it been so widely regarded as only trivial? The reputation of gossip for triviality may be explained by its social context. Typically, we expect people to gossip when they are at leisure, as part of what we call relaxation, entertainment, or recreation, while playing a game of cards, gabbing with fellow workers over a coffee break, or conversing at a party. We generally don't expect to hear gossip while people are hard at work, being totally productive, doing their best to get a job done. Similarly, we probably don't expect to read gossip on the front page of the *New York Times* or to see it repeated on a network newscast. On the other hand, the "Lifestyle" or "Entertainment" section of the local newspaper (near sports and comics) almost always contains a gossip column. This is the "less serious" section of a paper, in which "soft news" or "personality journalism" has a place.

Because of the influence of context, the same item may or may not be called gossip, depending on where it occurs. Two housewives discussing a teenage pregnancy over coffee are "gossiping." Two social workers having the same conversation about a client are hard at work. The housewives are doing something many regard as illegitimate; they are a couple of "busybodies" who have no other purpose in mind than to malign the reputation of someone down the block. Hence, we call what they are doing gossip. The two social workers are, by contrast, performing their role as social workers who feel responsible for the welfare of a client. What they say about others is part of their job.

Despite its reputation, gossip is sometimes our only way of obtaining accurate information. In the face of a press blackout, for example, gossip may tell us what is happening and why, who is doing what, and what we can expect in the future. After an earthquake devastates a region, for example, the survivors often spread information about the impact of the tragedy and the likelihood of additional casualities.

What is the difference, then, between gossip and news? In many cases, the only difference that actually exists may be their position in a newspaper. In other words, news is what you find on the front page; gossip is located in the "Living" section or in a supermarket tabloid. At the extreme, the dubious importance of a front-page article about the World Series is at least occasionally overshadowed by a story in the *National Enquirer* such as "Cuba's Castro Approves Plan to Export Heroin to the U.S." or "Computer Theft from Government Banks Reaches $1 Billion a Year."

In the popular image, however, news is treated as though it were substantiated or verified, based on several sources, whereas gossip is seen as completely unverified and unreliable. We expect to find on the front page of the *New York Times* (on the front page of any daily newspaper, but especially the *New York Times*), not unsubstantiated hearsay or unidentified second- and third-person accounts, but hard data based on direct observation or interviews with participants in an event.

In fact, however, much front-page news is based on an anonymous "reliable" source, and much of what we call gossip comes straight from the horse's mouth. Reporters are well aware that their success often requires keeping their "ears to the ground" and using the "grapevine" in an effective manner. Sometimes, however, the use of unnamed sources may lead to inaccuracy.

As a reporter for the *Washington Post*, twenty-six-year-old Janet Cooke received the Pulitzer Prize in 1980 for her story "Jimmy's World." In her front-page article, Cooke described an eight-year-old ghetto youngster whom she called Jimmie and who was given heroin injections by a drug pusher while his mother looked on. A few days after the prize was awarded, Ben Bradlee, the *Post*'s Executive Editor, learned that Cooke had lied about her educational background. She had not actually graduated from Vassar or received a master's degree from the University of Toledo, as she had claimed in the biography submitted to the Pulitzer judges. Nearly eleven hours later, Cooke tearfully confessed not only having exaggerated her credentials, but also having fabricated most of her Pulitzer Prize–winning article, including Jimmy.

The events leading to the discovery of Cooke's hoax began immediately after the publication of her story about "Jimmy." Fearing for the boy's safety, District of Columbia police threatened court action in order to force Cooke to reveal Jimmy's identity. Instead, the *Post* argued that the police demand was a violation of the First Amendment guaranteeing freedom of the press.

To locate Jimmy, the mayor of the District then formed a task force consisting of hundreds of police and social workers. After three weeks without success, however, the search was called off.

In the meantime, editors at the *Post* were also concerned for Jimmy's safety and asked Cooke to at least point out the boy's house to another reporter. But Cooke told them that she had already gone to Jimmy's home, only to discover that his family had moved after being threatened by the pusher. The editors' suspicions grew.

It was not unusual for *Post* editors to let a reporter write a story without revealing sources. Like most respectable newspapers, the *Post* was willing to protect its sources by permitting them to remain anonymous. In "Jimmy's World," Cooke had never identified her sources to her editors, but they saw no reason to question their authenticity. Cooke told the editors that Jimmy's drug dealer had threatened to kill her if she revealed her sources, even if only to them.

But editors around the country saw the *Post*'s handling of the Cooke story as inexcusable. Although few of their own newspapers had written policies on the use of unnamed sources, they argued that the *Post* editors should have insisted on being given the identity of Cooke's sources. This was especially important, they contended, because Cooke had been with the newspaper only a short period of time and had not proved her credibility.[25]

Unfortunately, Janet Cooke's fabrication was only one example of the improper use of anonymous sources by reporters on respectable newspapers. In an August 25, 1986, story, the *Wall Street Journal* suggested that Libyan leader Muammar Kaddafi was planning to support more terrorist attacks around the world and that the Reagan administration was preparing a second military strike against Libya "to teach the mercurial leader another lesson."[26] Following on the April bombing of the Libyan capital by the United States, the *Journal* story had the ring of truth to it, especially considering that it was based on the word of "high-level officials" and was not later denied by Reagan spokesman Larry Speakes.

In October 1986, however, Bob Woodward, writing in the *Washington Post*, revealed that the *Journal* article was part of a systematic U.S. government-sponsored "disinformation program" designed to destabilize Kaddafi's power by spreading false reports that the United States and Libya were on a "collision course." Moreover, though this disinformation campaign was intended primarily for consumption abroad, the White House apparently had done nothing to stop it from circulating to members of the American press as well.

Government-initiated disinformation is nothing new. Eisenhower lied about the downing of U-2 pilot Gary Powers, Kennedy lied about the Bay of Pigs, Johnson lied about Vietnam, Nixon lied about Watergate, and Carter lied about the abortive Iranian hostage raid. According to the Church Committee, which was established in the 1970s to investigate the Central Intelligence Agency, numerous unsuspecting newspapers have subscribed to foreign news services that were actually fronts for the Central Intelligence Agency. Thus, stories planted in other countries by the agency sometimes ended up on the front pages of local American papers and in nightly newscasts here.

According to Senator David Durenberger, the uncritical tendency of the American press in printing planted stories is a result of what he calls "scrambling for scoops." Reporters compete with one another to get an angle for an article, to get "the story behind the story."

*Newsweek* reporter Jonathan Alter sees the use of unnamed sources as contributing directly to the problem of planting propaganda. According to Alter, it is easy to plant stories when reporters depend so much on "high-ranking anonymous informants, many of whom ensnare reporters with promises of access and play-by-play insider detail." Referring to the Reagan administration's disinformation campaign, Alter reports that the *Wall Street Journal* article alone contained forty-two uses of "sources say," "officials say," and other variations.[27]

Just how prevalent is the use of unnamed sources in hard news? With the assistance of sociologist Lesli Overstreet, we examined the front page of the *New York Times* Sunday edition from October 1985 to September 1986.[28] Incredibly, she determined that as many as 70 percent of the front-page stories published during this period contained at least one anonymous source. Many were so vague that they could have been almost anyone: "sources familiar with the group's deliberations," "officials," "sources close to the investigation," "intelligence sources," "witnesses," "according to reports here," "a key official," "one law enforcement official," "critics," "campaign strategists," "government officials," "Indian officials," and "delegates." Some reporters even admitted to using second-hand sources or obtaining information over the phone from an unknown person. For example, in a story indicating that Reagan had accused the Soviets of sending arms to Managua, "officials said United States intelligence sources had information showing that a Soviet freighter . . ." and

"The spokesman was in Nicaragua, according to the person who answered the phone, and no one else could respond."

The distinction between gossip and news breaks down completely in what historian Robert Darnton has referred to as an underground system of "para-news," which seems to operate where censorship does not permit open discussion of public issues and public figures. At the time of Louis XV, gossip was spoken, sung, written, and printed. Censorship laws did not permit newspapers, but gossips wrote their illegal tidbits on manuscript news sheets, which were then distributed "under the cloak" in local cafés and public gardens. The juiciest gossip often was put into rhyme and was adapted to popular songs (for example, to the tune of "The Bear Went over the Mountain"). Some of it was finally published in underground scandal sheets.

Wherever an authoritarian press exists for the purpose of supporting the government in power, gossip will provide citizens with the news they might otherwise never obtain. In the Soviet Union, for example, the formal channels of news and information are totally controlled by the government. (Under the communist theory, the press exists in order to represent the viewpoint of the "government of the proletariat.") Yet, Russian citizens manage somehow to gain access to nongovernment sources of news. They learn about regional, national, and international affairs through gossip and rumor—through everyday conversation, forbidden books and articles, and the "underground" circulation of notes and manuscripts. Many Russian citizens have little or no exposure to official mass media; they rely instead on a thriving "rumor factory" to supplement, correct, and offset government propaganda.

As we have seen, the gossip found where we expect it—in gossip columns and supermarket tabloids—is predictably trivial and mundane, and often surprisingly flattering. If we had ended our investigation of gossip with its obvious forms, we might have concluded that gossip is generally a positive force in mass culture, relieving people of their daily tensions. Even everyday gossip contains a large share of positive information about other people's lives.

But gossip also exists where we least expect it. In fact, in its most insidious forms, we don't call it by that name. Drew Pearson, for example, was for decades a Washington political columnist, perhaps better known as an investigative reporter. Few would say he qualified as a professional gossip; he didn't appear in the "Lifestyles" section of the daily newspaper or in a supermarket tabloid. Yet much of his column was, in fact, devoted to gossip, often very negative gossip, about people on the Washington scene. He practiced what might be called "verbal voodoo" on Washington political figures by using gossip as a weapon against them.

The methods Pearson employed to gather evidence against his enemies were precisely those of the best gossip columnists of his day, especially Parsons and Winchell. Like his counterparts in Hollywood, Pearson also "went native" by attending the social events of the celebrities about whom he wrote. Rather than actors, directors, and writers, however, he rubbed shoulders with Senators, Representatives, and expensive political advisers, often over lunch, dinner, or cocktails.

A single entry in his diary for April 21, 1956, suggests just how important this approach could be:

April 21: Televised all A.M. Lunched at the Rid-
ders'. Senator Knowland was there and found myself
at the same table with him and Helen Knowland, both
swell people personally. Whenever I talk to her, I
wonder why she wanted to take sleeping pills as she
did in a suicide attempt two years ago. Yet it's probably tough living with the Senator—about as tough
as living with a columnist. He thinks Kefauver will
probably carry California—depending on whether he
first carries Florida.

Went to the big Democratic dinner. Lots of
Democrats were sore at me because of Wednesday's
column in which I said the dinner was going to be a
flop. It was Ernie Cuneo who wanted me to write the
story and it was Ernie who more than anyone kept
the dinner from being a flop. It was pretty dreary at
that.

Afterward we went to a party given by Phil
Stern, Research Director for the Democratic Party
Headquarters. Harriman was there, looking quite
young: invited me to come up to Albany again. I must
say that when you get a bunch of Democrats together
they have so much more on the ball than the Repub-
licans that you wish for old times again.

Carmine DiSapio told me Estes made a mistake
when he challenged the Meyner machine in New Jersey. He should have confined his campaign to south-
ern farm areas where Meyner is weak.[29]

As we have seen, gossip columnists often depend
on informants. Throughout his long career, Drew Pearson similarly loved receiving tips by telephone and in
face-to-face interviews. For information about politicians
that would otherwise have been inaccessible, he also
depended on the resources of organizations such as the
Anti-Defamation League, which were eager to expose

right-wing radicals. At one point, Pearson took a more "proactive" stance by hiring as his investigator a former prohibition undercover agent.

Jack Anderson, a former Mormon missionary who became Pearson's junior partner in later years, tended to keep his distance from politicians. When he took over "Washington Merry-Go-Round" after Pearson's death, Anderson told his assistants to avoid White House cocktail parties and dinners with informants. In the tradition of his mentor, however, Anderson was able to produce a number of exclusives that enhanced his reputation, including the printing of the Pentagon Papers revelations and President Nixon's personal bias in the Indian-Pakistani War.

In 1969, columnist Jack Anderson pressed his investigation into the tragic death of Mary Jo Kopechne on Chappaquiddick Island. As suggested earlier, Anderson's version of the story differed in essential aspects from that of Senator Ted Kennedy, who had left a number of unanswered questions in the minds of the press and the public about his role in the accident that caused Mary Jo's death.

Using an approach that his predecessor had perfected, Anderson claimed to have obtained his information about Chappaquiddick from Ted Kennedy's close friends. According to Anderson, "All have been extremely reluctant to talk. You talk to one close friend and after great effort you get one fact out of him. Then you go to another guy with the one fact and get him to elaborate on it. Sometimes, I'd call one and say something outrageous. Then, in the process of denying it, he'd volunteer a fact I didn't already know."[30]

More than any of his associates in Washington, Pearson used gossip as an effective weapon, sometimes as blackmail, against the politicians whose views or voting records he despised. Any Senator who voted against a bill that Pearson supported could rest assured that the nastier aspects of his or her private life would be printed in the next morning's edition of "Washington Merry-Go-Round." A Representative who espoused a political ideology at variance with that of Pearson might easily become a permanent target for Pearson's column, being "exposed" on a regular basis.

In Washington, Pearson made a difference. Four Representatives went to prison and a Senator was censured on the basis of Pearson's accounts of their financial misdeeds. His column reported that one member of Congress had a dead man on his payroll and that the son of another was involved in a paternity suit. He identified Senators who had been supplied mistresses by British intelligence, who delivered ghost-written speeches, and who engaged in "ghost voting," that is, the practice of having their vote on a bill recorded though they had not been present to vote. In addition, he attacked members of Congress in his column for everything from violent behavior, junketing, and absenteeism to alcoholism. He saved his most vicious attacks for his enemies, those, for instance, who opposed Medicare, oil-pipeline safety, aid to Appalachia or city slums, or improved meat inspection. Interestingly, as in other forms of gossip, his ends might have been laudable, but his means left much to be desired.

Sometimes, Pearson's use of gossip as a weapon was obvious. When, for example, Senator McKellar of Tennessee harassed a project highly valued by Pearson, the Tennessee Valley Authority, he was criticized in "Washington Merry-Go-Round" for brandishing a knife at another Senator. Pearson's staff would warn members of Congress that a vote against one of his "pet" projects or policies would result in their names' appearing in his column, "along with provocative comment about other misdeeds, such as loading a nephew on the payroll, touring the Paris nightclubs at government expense, or chasing a secretary around a table in the office."[31]

Pearson wasn't the only person in Washington who knew the power of gossip and scandal. Federal Bureau of Investigation Director J. Edgar Hoover was intimately familiar with gossip as a weapon, employing it with varying degrees of effectiveness against those he considered his political or ideological enemies. In 1966, for example, it was discovered that the telephone of civil rights leader Martin Luther King, Jr., had been tapped, apparently by Hoover. As director of the FBI, he certainly had the power to initiate an unauthorized wiretap. Moreover, his long record of "questionable racial attitudes" made him a prime suspect.

Hoover was no friend of the civil rights movement. Few of his agents were black, and he had been accused for decades of harboring antiblack sentiment, if not out-and-out racism. Hoover especially hated the leaders of the civil rights movement. In one interview, the FBI director later confessed about Dr. King, "I held him in complete contempt because of the things he said and because of his conduct."[32]

Hoover's hostility may have led him to launch a thorough investigation into the sex life of Dr. King and other popular civil rights leaders. He had originally demanded the right to "bug" King, in order to gain evidence that the popular black leader was associating with "hard-core, controlled Communists." Unable to prove his allegations, however, he instead began calling Dr. King a "moral degenerate."[33]

In one of many memos sent to President Johnson, Hoover reported that a prominent civil rights leader was having an illicit love affair with a woman from Los Angeles. According to Hoover, the civil rights leader telephoned the woman every week and had met her clandestinely in a number of cities across the country. Hoover reported one incident in which the man attended a party held in a New York hotel. Intoxicated, he had threatened to jump from the window on the thirteenth floor of the hotel if his lover didn't say she loved him.

Was Hoover talking about Martin Luther King? Although conclusive proof was lacking at the time of the report, the story, as later "leaked" to the press, left the clear impression that Dr. King was sexually promiscuous. One writer quoted a former official of the Justice Department as remarking about Hoover, "You couldn't spend thirty minutes with him without his bringing up the sex thing about Dr. King."[34]

Hoover attempted to discredit Martin Luther King by snooping into his personal life via taps and bugs. But when the story of his efforts to spread vicious gossip about Dr. King was revealed, Hoover's own credibility became imperiled. The public became increasingly concerned about Hoover's apparently unchecked power to defame anyone he disliked. As suggested in one newspaper editorial, "The King case is a frightening example of how political police can misuse their powers with the help of electronic gadgetry and huge files."[35]

Gossip has made front-page headlines and network news. During the summer of 1982, CBS News ran a story about two teenaged former Capitol Hill pages who alleged, under the cloak of anonymity, that unnamed members of Congress had seduced them. Despite "eyewitness testimony," however, an investigation by the House Ethics Committee concluded, "These allegations resulted either from out-and-out fabrication, overactive teenage imagination stimulated by conversations with a journalist, or teenage gossip which has in virtually every case proved to be utterly inaccurate."[36]

Maybe so, but in July of the following year, the same Ethics Committee recommended that the full House "reprimand" two Representatives, Democrat Gerry Studds of Massachusetts and Republican Daniel Crane of Illinois, charging that they had engaged in sexual liaisons with pages in 1973 and 1980, respectively. The House went beyond the committee's recommendation by voting overwhelmingly to censure, not simply reprimand, both members. For Representative Crane, the distinction made little if any difference. For Studds, however, the censure meant that he was automatically stripped of his subcommittee chairmanship.

According to the special counsel's report, Studds had had a sexual relationship with the male page just after Studds's election to the House. He first invited the seventeen-year-old boy to dinner at his Georgetown apartment, where they drank Cape Codders and spent the night together. Later that year, Studds took his young companion on a two-week trip to Portugal. The page later testified that he had been neither coerced, threatened, nor damaged; that "essentially all I needed to do to stop the relationship was walk out the door."[37]

The probe also found that Crane and a seventeen-year-old female page had had sex four or five times, beginning a year or so after Crane had come to Capitol Hill. In their first encounter, Crane and the page wagered a six-pack of beer on the score of a basketball game. To pay off the bet, she accompanied Crane to a bar in Virginia but was refused service because she was underage. They then went to Crane's suburban apartment, where they slept together. According to the page, she "found the Congressman as an older man very attractive" and admitted being "perhaps . . . more responsible for the sexual relationship than he was."[38]

Both Representatives admitted their transgressions. In an "extraordinary speech" on the floor of the House, Studds confessed being gay. He also granted that he was wrong to have had sex with a congressional subordinate, and that he had made "a very serious error in judgment." Crane was more apologetic, saying in a written statement, "I'm sorry that I made a mistake. I'm human, and in no way did I violate my oath of office. I only hope my wife and children will forgive me."[39] At a news conference, accompanied by his wife and daughter, Crane tearfully addressed his constituents: "I've broken the law of God, and I can only ask for God's forgiveness, my wife's forgiveness and my friends'."[40]

Crane's press secretary tried to play down the significance of the congressional censure. "If we required the resignation of all Congressmen who slept with young ladies," he asserted, "we wouldn't have a Congress."[41] He later retracted the statement. He was also proved wrong by the results of the next congressional election, in which Representative Crane lost his seat.

The relatively harsh treatment of Crane by his home-state constituents may have been triggered by his public image as a hard-line, tough-minded, old-fashioned conservative. Just one year earlier, for example, he had sent out a fund-raising letter in which he decried moral laxness in the country. All of a sudden, he was viewed by at least some downstate, Bible-belt Illinois voters as a self-proclaimed hypocrite who had "broken the law of God."[42]

Studds apparently fared much better than Crane, at least in his home state. The reaction in his Massachusetts district was largely sympathetic, even among the blue-collar workers of New Bedford, who seemed more concerned about their Representative's ability to protect jobs than about his personal life. Indeed, Studds's decision to "come out of the closet" was applauded by members of the heavily gay community of Provincetown on Cape Cod. One gay organization contributed $10,000 to his reelection campaign. Upon returning to his district for the first time since his censure, Studds was greeted by an enthusiastic, cheering crowd of some ten thousand people.[43]

One of Studds's rivals for the Democratic nomination tried to raise the House censure as a campaign issue, which he called "an act of child molestation." But the voters apparently didn't agree; they sent Studds back to Congress for another term.[44]

Perhaps we can better understand the harsher reaction to Crane's transgression by examining the case of another conservative member of Congress. Until the fall of 1980, Bob Bauman was a Republican representative from Maryland who anticipated his reelection that November. However, a scandal about Bauman became public just before this election—a scandal involving gossip so damaging that he went on to lose his seat in the House, his wife, and his law practice.

The most widely published account of Bauman's behavior was based on an "official government memorandum" that stated that during the winter of 1979–1980, he had solicited sexual favors for fifty dollars from a sixteen-year-old nude male dancer at a Washington, D.C., gay bar called the Chesapeake House. Another version of this story appeared on the front page of the *Washington Post*. It indicated that, as part of its pornography investigation, the FBI had accidentally come across a young man who claimed that he had had sex with Bauman, and that he gave his report as a way of getting out of his own troubles with the law.

Although nine other members of the Senate and House were also being investigated for homosexual conduct, Bauman was singled out and charged with the criminal misdemeanor of solicitation for prostitution. According to Bauman, his "chief antagonist in the House political war"—Tip O'Neill—gave official and political approval to pursue his case. A major FBI investigation was then initiated on the private sex life of Bauman: "Agents fanned out over Washington and surrounding areas interviewing every male hustler they could find, asking if they knew me (showing them my photo) and if so, had they ever had sex with me. Arrangements were made with a Chesapeake House employee to notify the FBI if I came into the bar. I was followed leaving the House office building some evenings and night photography was used."[45]

Bauman claimed that the FBI case against him was based on gossip from dubious witnesses. One such source of gossip was Eddie Regina, a twenty-six-year-old male prostitute who was also a paid informant for the FBI. Certain that reports from people like Regina would destroy Bauman's reputation and political career, Bauman's lawyer tried to prevent a courtroom appearance but failed. According to one U.S. Attorney's staff member, "The people of Bauman's congressional district have a right to know what kind of man he is before they cast their votes."[46]

Bauman's lawyer responded by arguing that the charges against Bauman were an attempt to use the court for "a political lynching."[47] Any political motivation was strongly denied. A request for court proceedings to be conducted in closed session was also denied, and Bauman was required to make a "public statement" in which he would make "full disclosure of the facts."[48]

The day before Bauman was to appear in court, a thirty-page FBI investigative memorandum, access to which he had been denied, was given to *Washington Post* reporters. The October 5 *Baltimore Sun* observed, "Mr. Bauman's lawyer, Mr. O'Malley, reacted angrily to the reports disclosing details of the FBI's investigation, material which he said was never presented to him in his discussions with the U.S. Attorney's office. . . . during those negotiations prosecutors presented him with no documents and no witnesses to substantiate the allegations (in the FBI report), only generalizations. They were extremely vague."[49] In other words, Bauman's lawyer charged that the government's case was little more than gossip.

Bauman came to believe that people in the Carter administration were intentionally leaking this gossip about his private conduct to sabotage his reelection, despite their claim that they only wanted to prevent blackmail of Bauman. Bauman maintained that they really wanted to end his "irritating public career": "Here was a chance to remove one of the most vociferous critics of the President, of his hapless brother, of his unpopular gasoline tax, of his confused energy policy, and of his floundering administration in general."[50] Bauman was also a "New Right" congressional leader and long-time Reagan supporter "who inflicted massive political irritation on the Honorable 'Tip' O'Neill."[51]

Although many of the "sensational charges" against Bauman could not be proved in court, they were widely publicized. As Bauman argued, "I seriously doubt that those bent on prosecuting me ever intended that the matter be handled quietly, in spite of their specific assurances to the contrary. Their purpose was not strict and impartial application of the law, but rather to make sure that my personal conduct was exposed before the 1980 election."[52] Bauman also contended, as further proof of political sabotage, that the FBI investigation conducted on him had been finished some eight months before election time. Despite this, the case against him was not brought up until sixty days before the voters were to decide Bauman's political fate.

As election day drew closer, the *Washington Post* featured an article about Bauman based entirely on a "confidential" memorandum written by Carol Bruce of the U.S. Attorney's office. The article quoted "all the juicy, lurid details including such phrases as 'closet homosexual' and 'pederast,' 'blackmail' and 'extortion,' 'violation of public trust' and 'abuse of public office.' "[53]

Bruce denied that she knew anything about how the leak had occurred. Other newspapers carried front-page stories about Bauman's private life. The *Baltimore News American*, for instance, reported that Craig Howell, a young federal employee, had seen Bauman in the Chesapeake House. *Washington Post* columnist Judy Mann described Bauman as having been caught "with his pants down."[54]

The press and news media pursued the Bauman scandal, creating "a major press circus." In one case, Bauman negotiated the facts of the story with the editor of the *Washington Post* to reflect what Bauman regarded as a "more factual" story. He also cooperated with a "friendly reporter" who was an editor of the *Baltimore Sun*, so his side of the story would also appear in the press. It did as a lead story in the *Sun*. Looking back on "his side" of the story, Bauman later admitted it was a "masterpiece of self-deception." No mention was made of his homosexuality; only his alcoholism was noted.[55]

Based on the gossip coming out about Bauman, articles on editorial pages appeared calling for Bauman's resignation (Bill Buckley in the *National Review*) or not (a *Baltimore Sun* lead editorial). All these articles were based on gossip and continued to discuss Bauman's personal life in an evaluative way. One newspaper, the *Daily Times* of Salisbury, Maryland, called for his immediate resignation and began a daily crusade to destroy him, contended Bauman: "Any story on the wires or in the Washington and Baltimore press was reprinted, usually on the front page, often with an eight-column headline above the masthead. The editor injected comments and asides in the body of the news stories explaining the meaning of such novel words as 'pederast' and 'sodomy.' "[56]

As the election neared, Bauman grew increasingly concerned about whether his opponent, Roy Dyson, would exploit the gossip about him. Despite Dyson's assurances that he would not take advantage of Bauman's private life in the campaign, he did. As election day approached, "Dyson's attacks on me suddenly became openly personal."[57] Bauman lost the election.

Soon after, Bauman also lost his wife. She asked for a separation. Bauman found life tragic. He searched unsuccessfully for an appointment in the new Reagan administration. Nor did law firms want his association. He decided to run in the 1982 election for his old congressional seat but bowed out in the face of "a carefully orchestrated campaign of word-of-mouth rumors."[58]

As with Crane, Bauman's political career was destroyed by gossip and scandal. Both politicians lived in conservative districts and were well known for their staunchly conservative positions. Unlike Studds, both Crane and Bauman came across as hypocrites. The disjuncture between their public politics and their private lives was simply too severe for their constituents to ignore.

Bauman's fate also raises a more important question regarding the use of gossip in politics. His downfall may have resulted not merely from an accidental disclosure but from a concerted effort on the part of his political opponents to discredit and disgrace his public image. Perhaps this effort explains why it was impossible for him to fight back with any effectiveness.

# Chapter 5    FIGHTING BACK

Imagine opening the daily paper and finding yourself featured in a syndicated gossip column. Suppose that, while passing through the checkout counter at a local drugstore, you see your photo plastered across the cover of a popular tabloid. What can you do about it?

Aside from bolstering the careers of Hollywood stars, some stories have "perks" attached to them. In recent issues of the *Enquirer*, for example, the tabloid arranged for celebrities to live out their fantasies, such as be a passenger in a hot-air balloon, the pilot of a Goodyear blimp and an F-4 jet fighter, a Las Vegas showgirl for a day, and the driver of a Formula-Four race car.

Janet Charlton of the *Star* claims that many celebrities "get a kick" out of the publicity she gives them in her column. Some have told her that the response from people they know has been "wonderful." For instance, she did a series of Rock Hudson stories: "People close to Rock Hudson said that they were the most truthful of anything printed about him in his final days. They were surprised at how accurate it was. . . . I ran into Pee Wee Herman at a party. He was delighted I had written about him. I like that. You know, some people are appreciative."

As is to be expected, not all gossip in columns and tabloids is met with glowing praise. Drew Pearson's controversial column often drew fire from Washington politicians, sometimes from the floor of the U.S. Senate. At one time or another, Pearson was described as "an infamous liar," "a lying ass," and "a dishonest, ignorant, corrupt and groveling crook." After being charged by the columnist with supporting subsidies to large oil companies and opposing them for poor farmers, a Senator from Georgia called Pearson "an ordinary, congenital, deliberate and malicious liar."[1]

In 1968, sixty-six-year-old Senator Strom Thurmond of South Carolina—a segregationist leader—married his twenty-two-year-old sweetheart. Shortly after the wedding, Pearson wrote in his column that "Strom and his Nancy are spatting." In response, Senator Thurmond told the press that the columnist had developed "a case of journalistic leprosy."[2]

Pearson's longest-standing feud was with Joseph McCarthy, the U.S. Senator who, in 1950, first charged that 205 members of the Communist Party were working in the U.S. State Department. In response, Pearson did a thorough background check on McCarthy's suspects, concluding that the loyalty of only three of them was actually open to question. Pearson also showed that two of the three no longer worked for the State Department, having resigned years earlier, and that one had never worked there at all.

Pearson consistently followed Senator McCarthy's vituperative allegations with accusations of his own, except that Pearson's were directed against the Senator himself. In some cases, McCarthy responded with characteristic viciousness. For example, Pearson reported that McCarthy had taken $10,000 from a housing organization in payment for a report of what amounted to merely a few pages. According to Pearson, the Senator was actually being paid off for his vote on the Banking and Currency Committee.

McCarthy was furious. At a supper-dance party to which they were both invited, the Senator accosted Pearson in the lobby, kneeing him in the groin and landing with a punch to the left ear. Twenty-four hours later, McCarthy described Pearson as he had described so many others: as "the diabolically clever voice of international communism and a Moscow-directed character assassin."[3]

Columnists continue to antagonize their targets. More recently, Columnist Janet Charlton has received a number of letters and phone calls from celebrities to complain about what she has written about them. Some of them have contained threats. But according to Charlton, she is usually able to convince these celebrities that she meant no harm and that they should have a sense of humor about their celebrity status:

> Sometimes, I get someone ranting and raving; but I point out to them they are looking at something from the wrong point of view. Look at it as a reader.

You know, readers expect a big star to have idiosyncracies.

I wrote about Lana Turner once being late on the set because she was having her hair done and about her having a lot of big movie star demands. I said, "Look. This is what your readers expect of you. You're a major movie star. I don't think you should look at it in such a negative way." So, she calmed down. She said, "OK—The next time you do a story on me, give me a call." And, she hung up.

Some celebrities become outraged when they read what has been said about them, and they publicly attack the columnist or tabloid reporter responsible for the story. When Nathan began writing her column for the *Boston Herald*, she was criticized and even threatened. During her first week on the job, another local paper referred to her column as "a new low in journalism." Later that year, an irate local celebrity actually tackled her to the ground.

Legal avenues are also available to celebrities who have exhausted every other means. Some seek both vindication and retaliation through the courts. In a Los Angeles Superior Courtroom, for example, Carol Burnett finally got to tell her side of the story; namely, that the *National Enquirer* had printed "a pack of lies" when, in a 1976 article, it implied that she had been drunk and disorderly at a meeting with Henry Kissinger.

The March 2, 1976, gossip column headlined "Carol Burnett and Henry K. in Row" read:

> At a Washington restaurant, a boisterous Carol Burnett had a loud argument with another diner, Henry Kissinger. She traipsed around the place offering everyone a bite of her dessert. But Carol really raised eyebrows when she accidentally knocked a glass

of wine over one diner—and started giggling instead of apologizing. The guy wasn't amused and "accidentally" spilled a glass of water over Carol's dress.

Some celebrities might not have minded getting publicity, even bad publicity, in a supermarket tabloid that has millions of readers. But Carol Burnett had a special reason to be offended: both her parents had died because of alcohol, and the article, she felt, had undermined her credibility in her campaign against alcoholism. After learning about the *Enquirer* piece, "I started to cry," she said. "I started to shake; I started . . . and then I calmed down and called my lawyer, and said, 'These are bad guys; I'm going to sue.' "[4]

That had been five years earlier, but the actress-comedienne obviously continued to be disturbed. "It's like having a toothache for five years and finally getting an appointment with the dentist," Burnett said after learning that her $10-million libel trial would begin in a day or two.[5]

Burnett's jury trial was held in the Los Angeles Superior Court before Judge Peter Smith. Attorneys for the *National Enquirer* contended that the tabloid had acted in a responsible manner within the standards of the First Amendment to the Constitution. Information about the incident, they argued, had come from a source that *Enquirer* editors considered reliable. *Enquirer* reporters had attempted to confirm the story before running it. Moreover, the effect of a ruling for the actress could be to reduce the ability of all publications to report information about public figures. Several editors at the *Enquirer* testified that they had believed the article was accurate.

William Masterson, a lawyer for the *Enquirer*, never disputed the accuracy of the report. Instead, he claimed that Burnett had not suffered from the story and pointed out that, a few weeks later, on April 6, the tabloid had printed a retraction, admitting that the original article was untrue. It read:

> An item in this column on March 2 erroneously reported that Carol Burnett had an argument with Henry Kissinger at a Washington restaurant and became boisterous, disturbing other guests. We understand those events did not occur and we are sorry for any embarrassment our report may have caused Miss Burnett.

This retraction, Masterson argued, corrected any possible error and ensured that the actress would not suffer a loss of either reputation or earning power. According to the attorney, there were actually three key questions in the trial: "Was the item itself defamatory? Was the retraction clear, and did Carol Burnett suffer from the article?"[6]

Had the *National Enquirer* acted with malice and reckless disregard for the truth? The criterion of "malice" does not legally apply to obscure citizens, who must prove only that they have been unjustly defamed. So for you or me, it would be easier to sue for libel. As a public figure, however, Burnett was obligated under the terms of a 1964 U.S. Supreme Court ruling to prove not only that the tabloid had wrongly injured her, but also that it had reported the story knowing that it was false, or in reckless disregard of the truth.

As for the retraction, Judge Smith helped Burnett's case. Early in the trial, he ruled that the *National Enquirer* was a magazine rather than a newspaper. Under California law, newspapers, but not magazines, are exempt from punitive or general damages in libel cases if they print a

"timely retraction." This ruling clearly reduced the importance of the *Enquirer*'s subsequent retraction.[7] It also opened
the possibility of a judgment exceeding the $250,000 limit
imposed only on newspapers.[8]

Both Burnett and Kissinger denied the accuracy of
the story. Moreover, two employees of the restaurant, the
Rive Gauche, filed affidavits saying that they had earlier
told *Enquirer* reporters that their information about Burnett's being intoxicated was untrue. Burnett never denied
that she had spoken to Kissinger at the restaurant or that
she had had "two, maybe three," glasses of wine. But, she
testified, "They portrayed me as drunk."[9]

Burnett's attorney, Ed Bronson, called fifteen witnesses and presented eight depositions. Seven days later,
the *Enquirer* rested its case without calling any witnesses.
Based on what he called "the First Amendment issue,"
*Enquirer* attorney Masterson said in his closing arguments,
"I speak not only for a client but also for a principle, and
that is the freedom of the press—your right to know."[10]

After deliberating for more than two days, the
eleven-member jury ruled that the tabloid had published
false, defamatory information about Burnett and then voted
unanimously to award the actress $1.6 million in damages.
On May 12, Judge Peter Smith denied a motion by the
*Enquirer* for a new trial but cut the original libel award to
$800,000. The judge suggested that this amount might be
enough to deter the tabloid from publishing libelous information in the future without putting it out of business.
He also said that the defendant had shown "absolutely no
remorse for its misdeeds." In fact, the tipster who was
responsible for starting "this travesty," R. Couri Hay, had
later been promoted to gossip columnist on the *Enquirer*.[11]

"I'm very satisfied with the judge's decision," Burnett said. "I hope the *National Enquirer* has been taught a

lesson." Indeed, this was the first libel judgment ever obtained against the tabloid. This was quite a victory, considering that Burnett is a public figure.[12]

Some journalists expressed concern in the wake of the *Enquirer* decision that unfounded gossip printed by a few sloppy reporters might start a flood of libel cases over unserious articles. Their concern was not misplaced.

But members of the "respectable" press like Liz Smith reacted differently to the *Enquirer* verdict in the Carol Burnett case. "It is no precedent against the First Amendment," she said. "Responsible publishers, journalists, and columnists can go on being fair-minded and work with impunity."[13]

According to legal expert Rodney Smolla, the establishment press tried, in the wake of public opinion favorable to the verdict, to dissociate itself from supermarket tabloids like the *Enquirer*. But this response often contained elements of "elitism" and "shortsightedness." Before the Burnett decision, the *National Enquirer* had never lost a court case for libel. Moreover, mainstream publications of the 1980s had made their own mistakes, some of which rivaled, if not surpassed, the *Enquirer*'s shoddy treatment of Burnett.

In 1984, for example, Ariel Sharon, former Israeli Defense Minister, took *Time* magazine to court in a $50-million lawsuit, charging it had libeled him in an article that described the findings of an Israeli commission (the Kahan Commission) concerning the 1982 massacre of eight hundred Palestinians in West Beirut by Christian Phalangists. In its February 1983 article, *Time* charged that Sharon knew of the likelihood of the massacre in advance and implied that he may even have encouraged it.[14]

*Time*'s accusations were based on a "highly reliable" source, or so it seemed. In fact, a low-level *Time* reporter,

David Halevy, had merely inferred, in the absence of sub-
stantiating evidence, that Sharon had discussed the massacre before it had occurred. This was not the first time
that the *Time* reporter had been involved in controversy,
having erroneously reported in an earlier story that Prime
Minister Menachem Begin was in extremely bad health.

The presiding judge, Abraham Sofaer, gave the jury
three questions to answer: The first was whether or not
*Time* had defamed Sharon by indicating that he "actively
encouraged" the massacre of Palestinian civilians. The jury
decided in favor of Sharon that *Time*'s article was indeed
defamatory. Second, the jury was to decide whether
Sharon, before the massacre, had discussed the need for
the Phalangists to take revenge. Again, the jury decided
in Sharon's favor: he had not discussed the issue of revenge.
The third question was whether *Time* had had "serious
doubts" about the truth of the defamatory statements concerning Sharon before the article about him was published.
In this question, the jury decided in favor of *Time*, concluding that it had not acted with knowledge of falsity or
in reckless disregard of the truth. In a statement accom-
panying the verdict, however, the jury suggested that correspondent David Halevy had "acted negligently and
carelessly in reporting and verifying the information."[15]

Sharon claimed "a great moral victory," whereas
*Time* continued to maintain that the substance of its report
had been essentially correct. It apparently ignored the fact
of the jury's first two verdicts, indicating that *Time* had
been in error and had libeled Sharon.

According to Smolla, libel litigation has recently
exploded. Court decisions encourage libel plaintiffs by
loosening the criteria for considering someone a private
individual rather than a public figure. Plaintiffs also seem
more willing to pursue libel actions, even if the process

takes years of court activity. And juries seem ever more willing to grant gigantic awards. Smolla, who is a professor of law, argues that all of this hangs "like a litigation time bomb" over authors, publishers and broadcasters.[16]

When it comes to limiting libelous gossip, lawsuits have clearly made a difference in the past. In the 1950s, scandal magazines such as *Confidential* routinely printed "dirt" concerning the private lives of Hollywood celebrities. But in 1957, lawsuits by Robert Mitchum and heiress Doris Duke, among others, severely restricted *Confidential* magazine's "penchant for unfounded gossip."[17] After being hauled into court by the State of California on charges that it had published obscene and libelous material, *Confidential* eliminated most of its Hollywood exposés. As a result, its circulation dropped from more than 5 million to less than 300,000.

It is difficult, if not impossible, to measure the effect of the Burnett lawsuit against the *Enquirer*, even if it may have encouraged a number of other Hollywood figures to take the tabloid to court. More clearly, however, the threat of libel judgments generally may have pressured newspapers and magazines to be more careful about printing gossip. During the 1970s, the *Enquirer* established a fact-checking department in its Lantana, Florida, headquarters. For the first time, all gossip items were required to have at least two independent sources. According to Jonathan Lubell, a New York libel attorney, this effect may be seen more widely in "more checking and investigating before gossip is printed."[18]

Even in the absence of a new official policy handed down from executives in the top echelons of management, tabloid reporters themselves sense a change in how they are expected to do stories about celebrities. According to

Richard Taylor, celebrity reporter for the *Enquirer*, there has been a noticeable "softening in the paper over the last few years in terms of angles. Years ago, the front-page stories were very hard-angled—for example, Lucille Ball is a rotten mother or Mary Tyler Moore feels she pulled the trigger herself in her son's suicide. But after the Carol Burnett lawsuit, there were more items like Marsha Wallace—an old 'Newhart' star—who talked about her mastectomy. The stories seemed to be softer, less negative."

Tabloid reporters who perceive a reduced demand for "hard-angled" stories are able to recite at least a few legendary pieces that were written in the days before they joined the staff. Carol Burnett is only one example.

The truth of such rumors may be less important than the fact that they are passed along to new generations of reporters who come to believe in their validity. A reporter who repeats one of these stories typically uses a disclaimer such as "I've been told" or "I'd have to check this to be absolutely sure" or "This happened some time before I joined the paper." Whether or not it is true, such "tabloid folklore" may be used to illustrate how the tabloids have changed over the years and especially to socialize new reporters about what is now expected of them.

More legendary than the Carol Burnett case, for example, is an incident that purportedly occurred "around 1976" in which Robin Leach from "Lifestyles of the Rich and Famous" wrote an *Enquirer* article about Walter Cronkite's believing in UFOs. According to *Enquirer* reporters, the Robin Leach–Walter Cronkite episode caused a major transition in the paper. Editors realized they had to check things out. The embarrassment resulted in a significant increase in the budget for the research department.

We tend to think of gossip as verbal—as the messages that people say or write about other people. Yet, electronic media have made possible a new kind of gossip—visual gossip in the form of photographs, motion pictures, television, and video casettes—which can reveal the most intimate details of an individual's lifestyle or personality and preserve it for the world to see. According to the cliché, one picture is worth ten thousand words, and for celebrities, visual gossip may represent an invasion of privacy that was not possible before the invention of sophisticated photographic equipment.

Television shows such as "Lifestyles of the Rich and Famous" and, to a lesser degree, "60 Minutes" and "20/20" have made legitimate use of visual gossip for the purpose of informing and entertaining their audiences. Usually with the permission of a celebrity, such programs enter the mansions, country clubs, offices, and restaurants of the wealthy and successful, giving viewers an opportunity to experience vicariously lifestyles far beyond their economic means.

There are also the illegitimate uses of visual gossip; some end up in the courts. For example, a free-lance photographer, Ronald Galella, once kept Jackie Onassis and the Kennedy children under surveillance in a manner that profoundly altered their privacy. To get candid shots of his subjects, Galella used such tactics as hiding in bushes and suddenly jumping in their path as they walked by, driving a motorboat close to Onassis while she was swimming, and jumping in front of John Kennedy, Jr., as he rode his bike. Galella even paid doormen and servants to keep him apprised of the movements of the family.

In response, Onassis sued Galella, not for money but for a court order to stop his invasive tactics. Ruling in favor of Onassis, the judge ordered the photographer not to keep Onassis or the Kennedy children under surveillance and to keep a distance of 100 yards away from them at all times. The appellate court generally upheld the order of the lower court but reduced the minimum distances from 100 yards to 25 or 30 feet.

In 1982, Galella was found guilty of twelve violations of the court order by taking photographs within 25 feet of Ms. Onassis. Under the threat of a fine of $120,000 or a six-month prison sentence, he agreed to pay Onassis's legal fees of $10,000 and never again to photograph her.[19]

Clint Eastwood's gripe was different, but it also involved visual gossip. The cover of the April 13, 1982, issue of the *National Enquirer* contained a picture of Eastwood with the caption "Clint Eastwood in Love Triangle with Tanya Tucker." The story itself claimed that Eastwood was romantically involved with both singer Tucker and actress Sondra Locke, and that the two women were constantly vying for his affection. One of the women was depicted as publicly kissing, hugging, and cuddling with Eastwood, and the other as begging on her hands and knees for Eastwood to maintain their relationship.

In his libel suit, Eastwood argued that the *Enquirer* had maliciously printed an inaccurate story to disgrace him. He also argued that the *Enquirer* had violated his right of publicity by publishing his photograph and name on its cover without permission and by running television commercials for the *Enquirer* in which Eastwood's photo and name were featured. This, Eastwood claimed, was commercial exploitation of his name and likeness.

A number of entertainers and athletes have recently attempted, through the courts, to prevent the unauthorized use of their names and pictures for commercial purposes. For example, Johnny Carson sued the company that made "Here's Johnny Portable Toilets" for using the "Tonight Show" expression for the purpose of selling toilets.

Unlike these other cases, however, Eastwood's name and picture appeared not on a commercial or an advertisement, but on the cover of a major magazine, the *National Enquirer*. The story about Eastwood's romances was newsworthy. If there had been commercial exploitation of his identity, then it was the news itself that was being "sold," and the news belongs to no one.

According to Smolla, the law has always allowed this kind of "exploitation." To permit individuals to have property rights in their news value as personalities would make a free press impossible. But a California appellate court ruled that Eastwood's case against the *Enquirer* was valid. If the story about him had been published in reckless disregard of the truth, then the *Enquirer* could no longer claim that his name and picture were being used in connection with the news. After all, if the information about Eastwood was false, it was not actually news.

Not unlike their counterparts in supermarket tabloids, columnists have also found themselves at the receiving end of expensive lawsuits initiated by well-known people who claim that their reputations have been damaged in print or on the air. During the thirty-seven years he wrote about Washington politicians, Drew Pearson had at least 275 suits seeking more than $200 million in damages filed against him by generals, members of Congress, and attorneys general. In all this time, Pearson lost only a single case.

But even litigation that ultimately exonerates a columnist raises serious problems. It may be time-consuming and very expensive. At the very least, it is anxiety-provoking until the final decision is rendered. And that can take time and effort.

Columnist James Brady, whose gossip appears in *Advertising Age* and *Parade* magazine, is a busy man who hardly has time to fight expensive lawsuits. As careful as he may be, however, Brady has been sued, although never successfully. Sometimes, a suit against him reaches the courtroom; at other times, it gets settled informally. Always, it is a difficult procedure that a columnist like Brady would rather avoid. For example,

> I was sued three or four years ago by Bernie Cornfeld—an international businessman who fell foul of, I think, Swiss authorities and actually served time in jail and is sort of a hustler. *Forbes* magazine wrote a very funny story about Bernie Cornfeld coming back to America. This is after going to jail. He's a rather plump, middle-aged man. He immediately takes over a big Hollywood mansion and starts throwing parties; and beautiful girls without bikinis are jumping in and out of the pool; and everything else. And it's the good life. And a reporter is there from *Forbes* and Cornfeld is wandering around saying, "Have you had enough to drink? How about some more caviar? Have you met Tootsie here?" So, the *Forbes* guy gets it all down and I wrote a report on this for the *New York Post* on the op-ed page. I said, "The good life is still out there in California." I said, "We're all indebted to Mr. Cornfeld for showing us that there is a better way." Of course, it was all tongue in cheek. But I called him a fat, balding old hustler, so he sued Rupert Murdock, his company the *New York Post*, and me. Later, I was separated from the case by Cornfeld's lawyers. I was dropped. In any event, the final decision came down 3 or 4 months ago. It was very funny, because the judge said, "I must admit, having met Mr. Cornfeld, that he is indeed bald and plump and

swindler. Therefore, the truth is the ultimate defense
here; and I throw out the case."

It is one thing to be mentioned in a local gossip
column or a supermarket tabloid; it is quite another to find
yourself on the front page of the *New York Times* or in
*Newsweek*. As we have seen, front-page gossip can hurt; it
can, if permitted to go unchecked, even destroy a good
reputation or a career.

The Most Reverend Louis Gelineau, Roman Catholic Bishop of Providence, Rhode Island, knows this very
well, having been the victim of such widespread gossip.
For a period of more than one year, beginning in the spring
of 1985, he was the target of widespread gossip depicting
him in extremely unflattering terms. Allegations included
the suggestion that he had been questioned and arrested
by local police and was to be transferred from his diocese
in the Providence area. Though these charges were never
substantiated, they continued to spread far and wide. Some
believed that the negative stories may have reflected dissatisfaction with Bishop Gelineau's leadership or with the
stand of the church on abortion, homosexuality, or women.
Speculating about the source of the gossip, Gelineau himself suggested that "There might be a network of people
there who would like to hurt me."[20]

But there is reason to believe that the stories about
the Bishop may have originated in a general sense of anxiety and concern among the citizens of Providence about
the safety of their children. Before the gossip began to
circulate, three Roman Catholic priests from the Providence area had been charged with sexually assaulting
young boys. Also at that time, the principal of a local high
school was charged with having picked up a boy for the

purposes of engaging in prostitution. The Providence community was alive with speculation about the guilt or innocence of these defendants and about how widespread such acts of sexual deviance might actually be.

As if this weren't enough, Bishop Gelineau was perceived by some to be an enemy of gay rights. In August 1985, he expressed his staunch opposition to a local gay rights ordinance that appeared to be on the verge of passage but was later defeated. Thereafter, unfounded gossip concerning his alleged "deviant" behavior became more specific. He was now depicted as engaging in homosexual activities.

For many months, Bishop Gelineau ignored the gossip about him. In fact, he declined invitations to publicly deny the allegations, believing that if he simply continued to do his job, the truth would eventually win out. He was convinced that a public denial would only lend credibility to the stories. What happened instead was that the gossip gained momentum, so that the entire Providence community knew about it. Some even began to consider the possibility that it was accurate. After all, "Where there's smoke, there's fire."

On April 4, 1986, however, Bishop Gelineau held a news conference in the studios of the NBC television affiliate in Providence. Taking the allegations one at a time, he acknowledged on prime-time TV that they had caused him anguish but that there was "absolutely no foundation" to them. He discussed the church's stand on homosexuality, abortion, birth control, and male domination of the Catholic hierarchy. He also defended his diocese's handling of the excommunication of the local Planned Parenthood director.

According to Richard Dujardin, religion writer for the *Providence Journal-Bulletin*, the results were dramatic.

In fact, the negative gossip about Bishop Gelineau "practically vanished" in the wake of his televised interview. During the week following the telecast, for example, Dujardin received only two phone calls from newspaper readers who refused to believe the bishop's side of the story. After that, the calls disappeared altogether.

The circumstances surrounding the tales about Bishop Gelineau illustrate the effect of false and malicious gossip on an individual. We saw that he was eventually able to dead-end the stories by confronting them in a public forum. But what can be done when gossip victimizes an entire group of people?

During the summer of 1979, Entenmann's Bakery—the world's largest producer of fresh baked goods—began hearing accusations that it was owned by the Reverend Sun Myung Moon's Unification Church, the so-called Moonies. Actually, Entenmann's was owned at that time by Warner-Lambert Corporation until it was later purchased by General Foods.

By 1980, there were hundreds of customer complaints to the managers of retail stores that carried Entenmann's products. Churchgoers in New York, New Jersey, and Connecticut announced at their Sunday services that Entenmann's was owned by the Moonies. Church bulletins, letters to the editor, and callers to radio talk shows all warned about Moonie ownership of the bakery and advised everyone to boycott Entenmann's products.

In 1981, the Unification Church bought some property and entered the fishing industry in Gloucester, Massachusetts. The mayor of the town responded by expressing his outrage on local television and in newspapers, depicting the Moonies as a bunch of outsiders who were trying to take over the community and who engaged in unfair labor practices in competition with local fishermen. Rumors also circulated that the Unification Church had kidnaped and brainwashed children in order to secure converts to the faith. As a result, members of the church received harassing phone calls, and some of their mailboxes were reportedly bombed.

At this point, Entenmann's Bakery was inundated with accusations. One of its drivers was physically assaulted by an angry customer. Overall, the bakery's reputation suffered and its sales declined.

With the cooperation of rumor expert Fredrick Koenig and a public relations team, Entenmann's decided to make a concerted effort to put an end to the stories. The bakery put together a media campaign in the Boston area including a major press conference. In November 1981, the bakery's chairman, Robert Entenmann, and Frederick Koenig appeared together on radio and television. Robert Entenmann specifically addressed the inaccuracy and unfairness of the Moonie stories, and Koenig discussed rumors generally. Their campaign was so effective that the rumors almost immediately ended.

Both the experience of Bishop Gelineau and that of Entenmann's Bakery illustrate what can be done to combat false gossip once it has entered the rumor mill. In the words of Koenig, with media exposure, "the rumor becomes news."[21] As such, the story loses its attraction for those who were eager to pass it along: it will no longer produce the same "sensational" reaction because it is already widely known. It will no longer provide the basis for isolated, unpopular individuals to attract the attention of others. In fact, it may even make such individuals look ridiculous. After all, why repeat a story that has already been shown to be discredited?[22]

# Chapter 6     CONCLUSION

It is time that we put aside our old ideas about gossip. Clearly, it is much more than just the nasty small talk of women over the back fence. Everyone gossips, men and women alike. And much of what they say is positive and flattering. Even in newspaper columns and tabloids with a reputation for spreading the dirt, one finds little in the way of nasty or vicious content. Certainly, there are gossip reporters who have made mistakes, printed errors, and acted unethically. But even among the most notorious and powerful of the professional gossips, cases of unethical revelation and distortion have been the exception to the rule.

The positive message found in gossip seems to be well represented in several other forms of popular culture, including song lyrics, movie themes, and situation comedies on prime-time television. Observers have noted that popular culture or mass entertainment fails to educate its audience and encourages escapism. In this sense, gossip is an "opiate of the masses." Like other kinds of mass culture, it gives people hope for a better life, even when hope is unrealistic, and allows them to escape, if temporarily, the pressures and problems they face every day. In addition, gossip provides the members of our mass society with an "invisible neighborhood" where their heroes become good friends. When the celebrity gossip is severely negative, we may instead use a well-known entertainer or politician as a negative reference point against which our own problems tend to pale by comparison. We then feel better about ourselves.

Thus, gossip may be psychologically beneficial. Many of the people who serve as role models for our everyday achievements—Babe Ruth, John F. Kennedy, Marilyn Monroe, and so on—have become national heroes through their exposure in the mass media and in the talk of ordinary people. More important, some of these heroes, through the medium of gossip, have grown into legendary figures whose character or accomplishments are communicated from generation to generation. They have become part of what we call our culture.

When a situation is unclear and laden with anxiety, gossip may be transformed into rumor. That is, a message about other people that may begin in a neighbor's home or in a local newspaper enters a process in which it is changed—exaggerated, distorted, reduced in size, or lengthened—as it is passed along from person to person. The mass media often play a role in getting gossip into the rumor mill. When, for example, government secrecy decreases the information available through official sources, there tends to be an "explosion" of rumor by word of mouth as well as in press reports. Sometimes, such rumors are accurate; at other times, however, they bear little resemblance to reality.

Another misleading idea about gossip is that it is, by definition, trivial. This reputation for triviality is at least partially a result of where we expect to find gossip, for example, in the "unserious" sections of a newspaper, in a supermarket tabloid, or over a game of cards. Actually, gossip can be extremely important—but it isn't necessarily what we normally call gossip, and it isn't always buried in the back of the Sunday newspaper. Once we have put aside our misconceptions, we can recognize that gossip also occurs where the "serious" news is located: in the front-page headlines or political pages of our most respected daily newspapers.

In one sense, this kind of gossip is potentially dangerous because it allows hearsay to become the basis for what we believe to be "hard news." Not unlike the items in tabloids and gossip columns, front-page stories rely heavily on unidentified and ambiguous sources of information. In the early stages of collecting important, fast-breaking news, it may occasionally be necessary for a reporter to rely on the word of a well-placed, highly ranked official who wishes to remain anonymous. Given the importance of front-page articles, however, we can hardly afford the excessive use of any device, hearsay included, that would permit fabrication and fiction to pass for established fact. Unfortunately, the prevalence of the unidentified source on the front page of the daily newspaper has grown dramatically throughout the 1970s and 1980s.

In another sense, media gossip has been a positive force in American life, if not indispensable to the democratic process. As a form of public opinion, it acts to constrain the behavior of our political leaders and national celebrities by making it almost impossible for them to hide from their constituents, and by giving us the "inside scoop" on their unethical behavior. The careers of some of our most successful politicians have been damaged or destroyed by defamatory gossip. At the extreme, gossip has been used as a weapon to reduce the power of the political opposition.

Still, there seems to be a double standard for ethical behavior between celebrities, on the one hand, and ordinary people, on the other. We tolerate much greater immorality and incompetence from nationally known figures than we do from our next-door neighbors. Indeed, unless the evidence is of overwhelming wrongdoing, a discovery of transgression may actually enhance the public image of a well-liked politician or movie star. Gossip about a fallibility or weakness, when it is not too severe, only serves to arouse sympathy and compassion; it makes our heroes into flesh-and-blood human beings with whom we can readily identify.

In the 1960s, the double standard was extreme. Our political leaders were still regarded, almost like royalty, as paragons of virtue and exemplars for the ethical and intellectual standards we hoped to impart to our children. In this view, our leaders could and would do no wrong, and if they did, we would look the other way.

In the wake of Watergate, however, public naiveté gave way to widespread skepticism if not cynicism. Every politician was seen as a potential Nixon who had to be closely guarded, lest she or he abuse the privileges of office. Every Hollywood star was similarly regarded as possibly addicted to heroine and sexually promiscuous.

The growing demand for journalists to play a watchdog role in constraining the behavior of public figures has led reporters to try to scoop their competition. Increasingly, they are willing to promise anonymity to sources who might otherwise remain silent. In the face of government secrecy, this practice has unfortunately resulted in the indiscriminate use of hearsay as a method for securing news. In a sense, much front-page news has become a disguised form of gossip.

Even gossip columnists have been affected by a growing sense of public skepticism. It is no longer enough for columnists merely to describe what a celebrity does in her or his occupational role. More and more, they are asked to provide the intimate details of the private lives of their celebrity targets, to inform their readers about the qualities that make a politician, government official, or a Hollywood star a decent human being when he or she is not in the public eye. A large and growing number of "smear biographies"—so-called unauthorized accounts of the lives of such celebrities as Bing Crosby, Joan Crawford, John Belushi, Elvis Presley, and Frank Sinatra—may be an effective way to humiliate those public figures who fail to live up to public expectations. Though it may happen less often than we expect, gossip has been known to punish as well as reward.

Some journalists have expressed concern that unfounded gossip printed by a few sloppy reporters in disreputable publications may start a flood of libel cases. Apparently, their concern has not been misplaced. According to legal experts, libel litigation has recently exploded. A growing number of celebrities are taking publications to court, and the judgments are bigger than ever. More positively, the threat of libel judgments generally may have pressured newspapers and magazines to be more careful about the gossip they print.

It is difficult to combat false gossip once it has

entered the rumor mill. Silence often implies guilt. With media exposure, however, a story loses its attraction for those who were so eager to pass it along in order to enhance their reputation or to make friends. What was formerly unverified and little-known gossip suddenly becomes hard-core news. It loses its value because it is no longer the inside scoop.

# Appendix A   METHODS OF INQUIRY

Many of our conclusions regarding the content of gossip columns were based on samples of syndicated columns from the time intervals 1954–1955, 1964–1965, and 1974–1975. For each time period, the entire population of column titles published in Philadelphia newspapers was studied. In 1954–1955, the following columnists were examined: Earl Wilson, Dorothy Kilgallen, Jimmie Fidler, and Cholly Knickerbocker in the *Daily News*; Ed Sullivan, Walter Winchell, Louella Parsons, and Leonard Lyons in the *Inquirer*; and Hedda Hopper in the *Bulletin*. In 1964–1965, Earl Wilson, Dorothy Kilgallen, Harry Hefferman, Dick Kleiner, Vernon Scott, and Suzy were studied in the *Daily News*; Mike Connolly, Louella Parsons, Leonard Lyons, Robert Sylvester, Hy Gardner, Herb Stein, and Walter Winchell in the *Inquirer*; and Sheilah Graham, Hedda Hopper, and "Here and There" in the *Bulletin*. In 1974–1975, Earl Wilson and Hy Gardner were examined in the *Daily News*; Joyce Haber, Suzy, Maxine Cheshire, Betty Beale, "Personalities, Etc.," and "People in Entertainment" in the *Inquirer*; and Walter Scott, Marilyn Beck, and "TV Tattletales" in the *Bulletin*.

Two dates per column title were randomly selected within each time interval. Finally, the first twelve instances of gossip in each of the selected titles per date were examined. An instance of gossip was indicated by the presence of information about a well-known person. This procedure yielded a final sample of 495 instances of gossip.

By means of appropriate recording sheets and definitions of categories, each instance of gossip in the sample was coded for the following characteristics:

1. The sex, race, and occupation of the target of gossip
2. The social context in which the gossip occurred (e.g., biographical, relationship and romance, pregnancy and the birth of a child, occupational information, drug and alcohol use, illness, death, party or social affair, public appearance, and travel)
3. The normative orientation of the gossip (e.g., foreign-born, dating and marriage, homosexuality, occupational praise or disapproval, ostentatious display of wealth, use of power, herosim or perseverence, criminal activities, drug and alcohol use, violation of folk-ways, and legal involvement and the courts)

In addition, information regarding the format of the column and the columnist's approval or disapproval of a celebrity's behavior was recorded.

The final category systems were developed by means of extensive pretesting on a comparable sample of gossip columns. The intercoder reliability of all measures was tested by having three coders independently code twenty-three instances of gossip taken at random from the population of columns. With the use of a two-out-of-three criterion (i.e., two of the three coders agreed), agreement ranged from 91 percent to 100 percent. Total agreement (i.e., three of the three coders agreed) ranged from 61 percent to 96 percent.

We also content-analyzed a sample of articles taken from the four most widely circulated gossip tabloids—the *National Enquirer*, the *Star*, the *National Examiner*, and the *Globe*—during the six-month period from February to July 1983. For each month, one issue per title was selected at random. This procedure yielded a total sample of twenty-four issues—six per title. All of the articles (excluding those less than a half page in length) published in the selected issues were subjected to analysis ($N = 311$).

Using appropriate recording sheets and definitions of categories, we coded each article in the sample for the following characteristics:

1. The sex, race, age, celebrity status (celebrity vs. obscure), and occupation of the target of gossip
2. The tone of the gossip (negative/positive/negative situation with happy or hopeful conclusion)
3. The quality of the gossip (mundane or everyday vs. extraordinary or especially important)
4. The topic of the gossip (romance or personal problems: alcoholism, drug abuse, obesity, victim of crime, medical or psychological illness; unusual occurrences: courage, unusual gift, miracle; occupational facts: films, personal appearances, records)

The final category systems were developed by means of pretesting on a comparable sample of articles published in the tabloids under study. The intercoder reliability of all measures was tested by having three coders (including one of the authors, who subsequently coded the entire sample of articles) independently code ten articles taken at random from the sample of tabloids. Using a two-out-of-three criterion (i.e., at least two of the three coders agreed), agreement ranged from 90 percent to 100 percent.

To collect data concerning face-to-face gossip, we analyzed 194 instances of gossip as they occurred in the conversations of 76 male and 120 female college students at a large northeastern university. These data were collected by having trained observers overhear conversations in the student lounge.

Seventeen male and eighteen female two- or three-person conversations were rated by either of two observers—one male, the other female—who had been trained in the use of a recording sheet designed for data collection purposes. All data were collected during a weekday interval between 11 A.M. and 2 P.M. for a period of eight weeks. To eliminate the influence of the sex of the observer, the two observers each coded one half of the male and one half of the female conversations. The observers always collected data in the same section of the lounge, seated unobtrusively with their backs to the group whose conversation they were recording. For the sake of detail, conversations lasting less than three minutes were eliminated from consideration. During the eight-week data-collection phase of the study, there were always large numbers of students in the lounge (almost always more than fifty), so that an observer's presence never aroused suspicion.

An instance of gossip was indicated by the presence of conversation about any third person, whether present or absent from the group. The observer noted the following information on the recording sheet about each instance of gossip: (1) the amount of time spent discussing a target; (2) the sex of the target; (3) the subject of the gossip (e.g., friend, teacher, stranger, celebrity, family member, or politician); (4) the topic of gossip (e.g., sex, dating, politics, sports, or course work); (5) the tone (positive, negative, or mixed); and (6) the presence or absence of the target. In addition, each conversation was coded for the following characteristics: (1) the number of group members; (2) the sex of the group members; and (3) the percentage of conversation devoted to gossip.

The category systems were developed by means of extensive pretesting on conversations in the student lounge. The intercoder reliability of all measures was tested by having the two observers independently code ten instances of gossip from the same four conversations. Agreement between observers ranged from 60 percent to 100 percent.

To study the methods used by gossip reporters, we conducted fifteen personal interviews with regional and national columnists and reporters from newspapers, magazines, and tabloids. Most were face-to-face interviews in the offices and homes of our informants. Our subjects were told that we were writing a book on gossip and that we were specifically interested in how gossip reporters did their work.

The interview schedule (see Appendix B) provided enough structure to ensure that we would cover major issues relating to the work of gossip reporters, but it was sufficiently flexible and open-ended to allow the subjects to elaborate freely and to suggest ideas that we did not think to pursue. Virtually every interviewee was highly cooperative. Each generously shared time, information, and feelings with us; indeed, some were reinterviewed despite their demanding schedules.

Although it was obviously impossible to interview legendary gossip columnists, we made use of various secondary sources, including their autobiographies and biographies. We also spent time in the field visiting and observing the very settings where gossip is collected and produced. For example, one of the authors spent time informally observing and casually talking with the staff of the *National Enquirer* in its Lantana, Florida, headquarters.

# Appendix B  INTERVIEW SCHEDULE

I. ENTRY AND TRAINING

A. When you were in high school or college, did you ever
think of becoming a gossip columnist? Did you do any
journalistic work? What was your major in college? What
kind of work did you have before becoming a gossip
columnist?

B. When did you first want to become a gossip columnist?
Why?

C. How did you actually become a gossip columnist? How
did you get your first column? Do you remember any of
the material you used in your early columns? How did
you build your reputation as a gossip columnist?

D. Do you feel that any of the work you did before publishing your first gossip columns helped you train to become a good gossip columnist? In your opinion, is there any difference between training to become a street reporter and training to become a gossip columnist?

## II.  THE GOSSIPING PROFESSION

A. Do you feel that anyone could be a good gossip columnist if give the opportunity? If not, what does it take to be a good columnist? What makes for a good gossip columnist?

B. Do you feel there is a special body of knowledge and a set of skills that gossip columnists share with each other and recognize as the basis of their profession? Is this basis at all different from that of the journalism profession?

C. Do you feel that gossip columnists have an informal code of ethics or set of standards? If not, should they? Do you have your own code?

D. Are there any legendary gossip columnists, like Walter Winchell, who might be considered models or even heroes in your profession? What classic or contemporary gossip columnists (or journalists) do you admire? Why?

## III.  JUSTIFICATION AND IMAGE

A. Some people think that most gossip is either petty or mean, or both. What you you think?

B. Do you think this bad image reflects at all on the gossip columnist? Some people might say that making a living from gossip is not respectable. How would you respond?

C. Do you think it is important for newspapers to publish gossip columnists? Why? Do you think the columns provide a service to the public, and if so, what service? Do you think they provide news? If yes, what kind of news?

Do you think the columns provide entertainment to readers? Examples? Do you think the columns may provide any "therapeutic" benefit to readers?

D. Do you feel that there is any difference between street reporting—news journalism—and gossip columns?

E. Do you feel that there is more to your columns than just dirt? That is, do you try to get any of your own messages, beliefs, or ideas across to your readers about human nature. If yes, what?

F. Rona Barrett says that sometimes she feels like a "crusader" breaking through the "fascist secrecy" of people who "control the news." Do you ever feel this way?

G. Do you feel you are in competition with other columnists or reporters? If yes, with whom and over what? Is this competition friendly?

H. How is it that gossip has a time value? Is being the first columnist to scoop a story the most important aspect of the story besides its content? Does this pressure make it difficult to verify all your material?

## IV. METHOD AND MATERIAL

A. What kind of information about people do you look for? What do you consider juicy or hot material? Examples?

B. Do you ever not print juicy material? Why? Examples?

C. Do you have special informants? Do you have regular informants as well as some who provide information only once? How do you develop a pool of regular informants? Why do you think people are willing to become informants? What's in it for them? How many do you have? Do you develop special relationships with your informants? Could you guess roughly the proportion of your printed material that comes from informants?

D. Do press agents ever send you material? Is it for their

own clients or is it about anybody? How often can you use this sort of material? Do agents ever try to cultivate your friendship to have access to your column?

E.  How do you operate at a party to collect leads and gossip? Do you try to circulate in a certain way? Are there certain people you try to seek out? Why? Examples? Do you carry a tape recorder with you at parties? Is it hidden? Do you take notes at parties openly, secretively, or later when you get home?

F.  Are there other social events besides parties that you attend to get material? Why? What kind?

G.  Do you try to verify all your material before printing it? How? Are there ever times when you print something that isn't verified? Why?

## V.  SUBJECTS/VICTIMS

A.  Are you interested in publishing material on any celebrity, or are there certain kinds of celebrities (e.g., sports figures or politicians) whom you would prefer to get material on?

B.  Do you identify or empathize with the subjects of your column? If yes, over what? Examples?

C.  Rona Barrett says that, when she began her career, she knew she had to "take out after someone" at least once a month to become a successful columnist, but she found this hard at first because some of these people were her friends. She rationalized her nasty columns by seeing them as revenge for nasty things done to her by these people. Did you have to start your career this way, too? How did you justify it to yourself?

D.  How about encountering hostility from your subjects. Are there some people who avoid you at parties for fear of showing up in your column, or because of something said in your column? Examples? How often do you get heat from material you print? Examples? Have you ever been sued? Elaborate. Do you ever get nasty calls or letters? Examples?

# NOTES

## CHAPTER 1

1. R. B. Stirling, "Some Psychological Mechanisms Operative in Gossip," *Social Forces* 34 (1956): 262–267.
2. Jean E. Laird, *Gossip, Gossip, Gossip* (Liquori, MO: Liquori Publishers, 1980), 7, 9, 20.
3. As quoted in Bob Thomas, *Winchell* (Garden City, NY: Doubleday, 1971), 160.
4. Ann Landers, "Gossip: The Faceless Demon That Breaks Hearts and Ruins Careers," *Philadelphia Inquirer* (August 22, 1985): 23.
5. Sissela Bok, *Secrets* (New York: Vintage Books, 1983), 101.
6. Alexander Rysman, "How the 'Gossip' Became a Woman," *Journal of Communication* 27 (1977): 176–180.
7. Patricia Meyer Spacks, *Gossip* (New York: Knopf, 1985), 26.

8. Rysman.
9. James Mercer Garnett, *The Gossip's Manual* (Richmond: T. W. White, 1825), 361.
10. Rysman.
11. Anne Edwards, *Vivian Leigh: A Biography* (New York: Simon & Schuster, 1977).
12. Albert Goldman, from the journalism of Lawrence Schiller, *Ladies and Gentlemen—Lenny Bruce!!* (New York: Random House, 1971).
13. Lena Pepitone and William Stadiem, *Marilyn Monroe: Confidential* (New York: Simon & Schuster, 1979).
14. Priscilla Johnson McMillan, *Marina and Lee* (New York: Harper & Row, 1977).
15. Robina Lund, *The Getty I Knew* (Kansas City: Sheed Andrews & McMeel, 1977).
16. Margaret Trudeau, *Margaret Trudeau: Beyond Reason* (New York: Paddington Press, 1979).
17. Rosemary Clooney with Raymond Strait, *This for Remembrance: The Autobiography of Rosemary Clooney* (Chicago: Playboy Press Book, 1977).
18. David Gwyn, *Idi Amin: Death-Light of Africa* (Boston: Little, Brown, 1977).
19. A summary of our methods of inquiry is located in Appendix A.

## CHAPTER 2

1. As in other forms of communication, there are certain unwritten, informal rules for the expression of gossip that are shared by the members of society. For one thing, gossiping involves an informal agreement among participants—whether friends, neighbors, co-workers, or the like—to exchange information and opinions about people, even if those people happen to be absent. For a conversation to proceed, the situation itself must be defined as congenial for gossiping. This means that those present must get to

know one another well enough to realize that gossiping will be tolerated if not approved. They must also establish that the names of the people brought up in the conversation are recognizable to one another. Questions like "Do you know John's roommate?" must be asked before further information is shared (for example, "Did you hear that John's roommate is quitting school?") or before opinions are solicited about targets (for example, "What do you think of John's mother?").

Most people would agree that the validity of gossip does not have to be justified; indeed, to challenge the authenticity of gossip is usually prohibited. Instead, those who hear gossip may ask the gossipmonger to indicate the source of his or her message: "How did you know? Who told you?"

This rule concerning gossip may produce a gossip backlash: the possibility always exists for the target of gossip to find out that others are talking behind her back and even to learn the names of those who are spreading the dirt. One result may be for a target to ask for an apology, especially when the message is without fact, or even to threaten a lawsuit for defamation.

Rather than condoning gossip, certain people in certain situations see it as "not the thing to do." If someone were to gossip under such conditions, he or she might be made to feel awkward by a lack of response from others or by being admonished not to continue. In extreme cases, gossip might be seen as so incorrect as to be considered a form of stigmatized speech that "spoils" the definition of the situation and inhibits further conversation.

Since the beginning of the twentieth century, etiquette books have attempted to formalize the rules and regulations for gossiping in order to control and limit it. In the 1929 edition of *Good Manners* (New York: L. M. Garrity, p. 31), for example, the author claimed that people may be seen as having poor "talking manners" if they are seen as "gossipy." Gossiping was lumped, in this advice book, with telling off-color stories, saying things that hurt people's feelings, or chattering so incessantly that no one else can get a word in edgewise.

Another popular etiquette manual, in its discussion of proper conversation, listed gossip, along with age, money, politics, and religion, as "dangerous topics." "Certain subjects," warned the author, "have rightly earned the label 'dangerous' because it takes luck as well as diplomacy to deal with them deftly enough to avoid their inherent hazards." Also according to this author, it is easy for listeners to confuse "genuine interest in other people and their problems with gossip for its own sake." A gossip who "blabs" everything he or she knows will be thought of as egocentric: "He is playing a subtle, dual game—showing himself superior to his audience by having a juicy piece of inside information, and superior to the subject of the gossip as well, if the item has an edge of malice." To deflate a gossipmonger, one should challenge the authenticity of the talk by asking, "How do you know?" Finally, the author alerted the reader not to trust the gossiper with any confidences (Llewellyn Miller, *The Encyclopedia of Etiquette* [New York: Crown, 1967], 23).

Eleanor Roosevelt's *Book of Common Sense Etiquette* (New York: Macmillan, 1962, 153) has a different concern about gossip. In her discussion of the "Do's and don'ts of the suburban or village dweller," she noted that chatting over the back fence can be a fine and satisfying occupation—as long as it is kept within bounds. The gossip can easily become a bore, and people with manners realize that much of what they say is uninteresting to others. Roosevelt wrote, "Do not keep your neighbor, who has perhaps come out to hang the clothes or to do some little chore about the place, standing for half an hour listening to your sad tale of how unfairly the teacher graded one of your children, or how inconsiderate your husband is, or how your infected sinuses are torturing you. She has other things which she would rather be doing, yet if she is a courteous human being, she will find it difficult to walk away while your chatter is going full tilt."

*Esquire's Guide to Modern Etiquette* (Philadelphia: J. B. Lippincott, 1969, 87–89) covers special gossiping rules for men. It is acknowledged that when women gossip, they are forgiven if not seen as lovable. But when a man gossips, "he throws suspicion on his manhood as well as on his manners." One who does not want to be known as an "old woman" never volunteers information about other people and is always noncommittal when answering questions about them. Several negative advantages result: "No one will ever misquote you, if you haven't said anything to quote. No one will ever wonder if perhaps you are betraying a confidence, or put you down as someone it's best not to confide in. No one will put your little scrap of news to his wider knowledge of the principals to reach a conclusion you hadn't anticipated. No one will use you as a catalyst in a situation outside your control. And no one (including yourself) will have reason to fear your innocent running-off-at-the-mouth."

*Esquire's Guide* also indicates positive advantages to refraining from gossiping: "If you speak no evil, pretty soon you'll hear no evil; with no tales to carry, you'll be spared the temptation to gossip. For in this realm, ignorance is bliss."

The question of talk becomes subtler, according to *Esquire's Guide*, when one is on the receiving end of gossip. This manual contends that "ideally, you should not even listen to malicious remarks—silence is a form of assent—but practically, you have to decide when a good defense of your absent friend is going to be a bad offense to your gossiping friend." There is, however, one rule that is unbreakable in *Esquire*'s book: "Under no circumstances can you talk about a woman."

2. John Beard Haviland, *Gossip, Reputation, and Knowledge in Zinacantan* (Chicago: University of Chicago Press, 1977).

3. Ralph Rosnow and Gary Fine, "Inside Rumors," *Human Behavior* (1974): 64–68.

4. Lewis H. Lapham, Liz Smith, Barbara Howar, William F. Buckley, Jr., John Gross, Mark Crispin Miller, and Robert Darnton, "Gossiping About Gossip," *Harper's* 272 (1986): 46.

5. Gossip about Hitler's life was taken from Robert G. L. Waite, *The Psychopathic God: Adolf Hitler* (New York: Basic Books, 1977).

6. Jack Levin and Arnold Arluke, "An Exploratory Analysis of Sex Differences in Gossip," *Sex Roles* 12 (1985): 281–286.

7. Tomatsu Shibutani, *Improvised News: A Sociological Study of Rumor* (Indianapolis: Bobbs-Merrill, 1966).

8. John M. Roberts, "The Self-Management of Cultures." In *Explorations of Cultural Anthropology: Essays in Honor of George Peter Murdock*, ed. by Ward H. Goodenough (New York: McGraw-Hill, 1964).

9. Bruce A. Cox, "What Is Hopi Gossip about? Information Management and Hopi Factions," *Man* 5 (1970): 88–98.

10. Jan W. Kelly, "Storytelling in High-Tech Organizations: A Medium for Sharing Culture," *Journal of Applied Communication Research* 13 (1985): 45–58.

11. Max Gluckman, "Gossip and Scandal," *Current Anthropology* 4 (1963): 307–316.

12. Sally Engle Merry, "Rethinking Gossip and Scandal." In *Toward a General Theory of Social Control*, ed. by Donald Black (Orlando: Academic Press, 1984), 277.

13. Fredrick Koenig, *The Tulanian* (New Orleans: Tulane University, 1984), 27.

14. Josephine Lowman, "Some Gossip Actually Could Be Good for You," *Champagne-Urbana News Gazette* (June 1983): 4.

15. Fredrick Koenig, *Rumor in the Marketplace: The Social Psychology of Commercial Hearsay* (Dover, MA: Auburn House, 1985).

16. Gossip about Aristotle Onassis and Jackie Kennedy was obtained from Fred Sparks, *The $20,000,000 Honeymoon* (New York: Bernard Geis, 1970).

17. Gossip about Howard Hughes was taken from James Phelan, *Howard Hughes: The Hidden Years* (New York: Random House, 1976).

18. Gossip about Elvis Presley was taken from Albert Goldman, *Elvis* (New York: Avon, 1981).

19. Earl Wilson, *Sinatra* (New York: Signet, 1977).

20. Jerry M. Suls, "Gossip as Social Comparison," *Journal of Communication* 27 (1977): 164–168.

21. Gossip about J. Paul Getty was obtained from Robina Lund, *The Getty I Knew* (Kansas City: Sheed Andrews & McMeel, 1977).

22. Elliot Aronson, Ben Willerman, and Joanne Floyd, "The Effect of a Pratfall on Increasing Interpersonal Attractiveness," *Psychonomic Science* 4 (1966): 227–228.

23. Charles Higham, *Bette* (New York: Dell, 1981).

24. Rosemary Clooney with Raymond Strait, *This for Remembrance: The Autobiography of Rosemary Clooney* (Chicago: Playboy Press Book, 1977).

25. Christina Crawford, *Mommie Dearest* (New York: Berkley Books, 1978).

26. Bill Adler, *Elizabeth Taylor: Triumphs and Tragedies* (New York: Ace Books, 1982).

27. Gossip about Marilyn Monroe was taken from Lena Pepitone and William Stadiem, *Marilyn Monroe: Confidential* (New York: Simon & Schuster, 1979).

28. Jack D. Douglas, *Deviance and Respectability* (New York: Basic Books, 1970).

29. Linden L. Nelson and Spencer Kagan, "Competition: The Star-Spangled Scramble," *Psychology Today* (1972): 53–56, 90–91.

30. Goldman.

31. H. Roy Kaplan, *Lottery Winners: How They Won and How Winning Changed Their Lives* (New York: Barnes & Noble, 1978).

32. Gossip about Elizabeth Taylor was taken from Bill Adler.

33. David Niven, *Bring on the Empty Horses* (New York: Dell, 1975).

34. George Gerbner and Larry Gross, "The Scary World of TV's Heavy Viewer," *Psychology Today* (April 1976): 41–45; Nancy Buerkel-Rothfuss, "Soap Opera Viewing," *Journal of Communication* (Summer 1981): 108–116.

35. Muriel Cantor and Susanne Pingree, *The Soap Opera* (Beverly Hills, CA: Sage, 1983).

36. Gary A. Fine, "Social Components of Children's Gossip," *Journal of Communication* 27 (1977): 181–185.

37. Merry.

38. Gluckman.

39. Lapham, Smith, Howar, Buckley, Jr., Gross, Miller, and Darnton, 44.

40. Gordon Allport and Leo Postman, *The Psychology of Rumor* (New York: Holt, Rinehart & Winston, 1947).

41. Koenig, *Rumor in the Marketplace: The Social Psychology of Commercial Hearsay.*

42. H. I. Buckner, "A Theory of Rumor Transmission," *Public Opinion Quarterly* 29 (1965): 54–70.

43. Edgar Morin, *Rumour in Orléans* (New York: Random House, 1971).

44. Rather than beginning with innocent fantasies, gossip can originate in a deliberate scheme to discredit the members of a particular group. This is precisely what occurred in the aftermath of the brutal murder of the New Orleans police chief in 1890. Chief David Hennessey was cut down by five men who opened fire with shotguns and pistols. By the next morning, millions of people throughout the nation read in their newspapers that the prominent police chief had been shot down by the "Mafia," based only on the word of a captain in the New Orleans Police Department, who claimed that his dying friend had whispered that his assailants were "dagos."

This charge fed directly into a widespread fear among local residents about the Mafia in New Orleans. Without a shred of evidence, the mayor made public a list of "ninety-four Mafia murders" in New Orleans. He forgot to mention that these murders had taken place over a twenty-five year period and that the list had been compiled by including every homicide in the city with an Italian-sounding name. He also failed to indicate that ninety-one of the murders were still unsolved. Indeed, the mayor's assumption that the killers were Italian and Mafiosi was strictly speculation.

The events which followed the murder of Chief Hennessey were carefully orchestrated by forces in local politics and business who resented and despised the Italians' growing economic and political power. Plantation owners were alarmed that these Italians, who had originally worked the sugar fields for slave wages, were suddenly buying up cheap land. Moreover, Sicilian fishermen and peddlers, shortly off the boat from the old country, were seen by the business leaders of New Orleans as monopolizing the fruit, oyster, and fish industries of the city.

After the murder of Hennessey, nineteen Italians were arrested. The trial of the first nine defendants ended in a mistrial for three men and a verdict of "not guilty" for the other six. Even before the second round of trials could begin, an angry mob took matters into its own hands.

The ensuing riot was anything but spontaneous. The morning after the jury's verdict was given to the court, local newspapers carried an advertisement inviting the citizens of New Orleans to attend a mass meeting "to remedy the failure of justice in the Hennessey case." Among the sponsors of the ad and leaders of the meeting were wealthy landowners, political leaders, and a political boss with a long history of violence.

These were the men who led some twelve thousand New Orleanians to storm Parish Prison, where the defendants were being held. After being stirred up to a frenzy by these community leaders, the angry mob slaughtered eleven Italians, three of whom had been previously acquitted, three whose court appearance had ended in a mistrial, and five more who had never even been tried. Another eight men escaped by hiding themselves in closets or under mattresses in their cells.

The cause of the largest mass lynching in American history cannot be attributed to sheer crowd madness. There was, instead, a deliberate plan on the part of those who stood to gain to eliminate the competition from Italians in local agriculture and industry. Gossip was employed in order to convince the citizens of New Orleans of the righteousness of taking the law into their own hands. What began as a well-planned conspiracy became mass hysteria and trial by vicious gossip.

45. Koenig, *The Tulanian* 27.
46. Shibutani
47. Buckner.
48. Ralph L. Rosnow and Gary A. Fine, *Rumor and Gossip: The Social Psychology of Hearsay* (New York: Elsevier, 1976); Ralph L. Rosnow and Marianthi Georgoudi, "Killed by Idle Gossip: The Psychology of Small Talk." In *When Information*

*Counts*, ed. by Bernard Rubin (Lexington, MA: Heath, 1985), 59–73.

49. Lorna Marshall, "Sharing, Talking, and Giving," *Africa* 31 (1961): 231–249.

50. Elizabeth Colson, *The Makah Indians: A Study of an Indian Tribe in Modern American Society* (Manchester: Manchester University Press, 1953).

51. Clyde Kluckhohn, *Navaho Witchcraft* (Boston: Beacon Press, 1944).

52. Ralph L. Rosnow and Allan Kimmel, "Lives of a Rumor," *Psychology Today* (1979): 88–92.

53. Gary Lee, "Soviets Blame Human Error," *Boston Globe* (May 3, 1986): 1.

54. John M. Goshko, "US Forgery Specialist Is Subject of His Latest Probe," *Boston Globe* (August 20, 1986): 65.

55. "Deadly Meltdown," *Time* (May 12, 1986): 39.

56. "Brezhnev Reported Mildly Ill," *New York Times* (August 1, 1968): 1.

57. James F. Clarity, "Brezhnev Reported Sick, Cancels Trip to Rumania," *New York Times* (July 5, 1970): 2.

58. "Rumors on Red Square," *New York Times* (November 12, 1972): 1.

59. Flora Lewis, "Soviet and France Press for a 35-Nation Summit," *New York Times* (December 8, 1974): 1.

60. Christopher S. Wren, "Brezhnev Calls for Accord against 'Terrifying' Arms," *New York Times* (June 14, 1975): 1.

61. "Brezhnev Leaves Early Second Straight Day," *New York Times* (August 1, 1975): 56.

62. David Shipler, "Brezhnev-Giscard Talks Feed Moscow Rumor Mill," *New York Times* (October 17, 1975): 1; Malcolm W. Browne, "Brezhnev Asserts Slander in West Poisons Detente," *New York Times* (December 10, 1975): 1.

63. Bernard Gwertzman, "US-Soviet Arms Accord Tied to Brezhnev's Health," *New York Times* (January 25, 1976): 1.

64. "Health Problems of Brezhnev Given," *New York Times* (June 17, 1977): A8.

65. "Notes on People," *New York Times* (December 27, 1977): 2.

66. "Brezhnev-Schmidt Talks Indicate No Gains on Arms," *New York Times* (May 6, 1978): 1.
67. "Brezhnev Said to Have Bad Case of Influenza," *New York Times* (March 29, 1979): 2.
68. John F. Burns, "Soviet Leaders' Clinic Remains under Close Guard," *New York Times* (April 4, 1982): 14.
69. John F. Burns, "Brezhnev Is Dead in Soviet at Age 75," *New York Times* (November 11, 1982): A1.

## CHAPTER 3

1. The modern gossip column has its roots in the rip-roaring twenties; in the lifestyles of great stars of this decade such as Fatty Arbuckle, Charlie Chaplin, Douglas Fairbanks, Francis X. Bushman, Mary Pickford, and Gloria Swanson; and in the incredible popularity of Louella Parsons and Walter Winchell.

Winchell was the first celebrity gossip columnist on the East Coast. He was hired in 1924 by the *New York Graphic* for $100 a week to write play reviews, to do a Broadway column, to act as amusement editor, and to be a tipster at the city desk. But his tips, at first, were often rebuffed by the city editor: "Once he brought the information that an aging stage star was planning to leave his wife to marry the ingenue in his latest play. 'Has his wife filed suit for divorce?' the editor demanded of Winchell. 'No, but—' 'Then it isn't news,' grumbled the editor" (Bob Thomas, *Winchell*, Garden City, NY: Doubleday, 1971, p. 32).

Winchell's real interest lay in the column he called "Broadway Hearsay." In the course of writing this weekly column, he picked up bits and pieces of Broadway gossip. One day when he ran out of jokes or poems to fill his column, he started writing up the gossip he had collected. His first gossip column included the following items: "Helen Eby Brooks, widow of William Rock, has been plunging in Miami real estate . . . It's a girl at the Carter De Havens . . . Lenore Ulric paid $7 income tax . . . Fanny Brice is betting on the horses at Belmont . . . S. Jay Kaufman sails on the 16th via the *Berengaria* to be hitched to a Hungarian . . . Report has it that Lillian Lorraine has taken a husband again . . ." By 1929, Winchell was doing his column for the *New York Mirror* (Thomas, *Winchell*, p. 34).

As his popularity heightened, Winchell began lacing his column with the "intimacies" of imminent divorces and other scandals. He would run as many as nine thousand items a year, and he couldn't check the accuracy of every one of them. Instead, he used a system for publishing news that he suspected to be true. It allowed him to reveal things that the public wouldn't know until an official announcement was made—or might never know, as with a hushed-up scandal. He would hint at news that propriety or the libel laws would not permit him to report openly. Among the Winchell devices were the blind item ("What married producer of three Broadway musicals pays rent for a chorus girl in each?"), the pointed question ("Are the Clark Gables seeing a lawyer?"), and the ambiguous phrase ("Billy Rose and Eleanor Holm are on the verge").

2. Thomas Wood, "The First Lady of Hollywood," *Saturday Evening Post* (July 15, 1939): 25.

3. Ezra Goodman, *The Fifty Year Decline and Fall of Hollywood* (New York: Macfadden Books, 1962), 30.

4. Ibid., 42.

5. Bob Thomas, *Winchell* (Garden City, NY: Doubleday, 1971); Herman Klurfeld, *Winchell, His Life and Times* (New York: Praeger, 1976).

6. Louella O. Parsons, *Tell It to Louella* (New York: Putnam, 1961), 316.

7. Unless otherwise specified, quotes from gossip columnists and reporters throughout this book were obtained from personal interviews.

8. Much of our evidence concerning the content of gossip columns was derived from Jack Levin and Allan J. Kimmel,

"Gossip Columns: Media Small Talk," *Journal of Communication* 27 (1977): 169–175.

9. The study of *People* magazine reported here was from an unpublished manuscript by Joyce Ruscitti at Northeastern University, 1985.

10. Much of our evidence concerning the content of supermarket tabloids was taken from Jack Levin, Amita Mody-Desbareau, and Arnold Arluke, *The Gossip Tabloid as an Agent of Social Control*, a paper presented at the annual meetings of the American Sociological Association, 1986.

11. Lewis H. Lapham, Liz Smith, Barbara Howar, William F. Buckley, Jr., John Gross, Mark Crispin Miller, and Robert Darnton, "Gossiping about Gossip," *Harper's* 272 (1986): 40.

12. Goodman.

13. Klurfeld.

14. Goodman, 41.

15. Steven M. L. Aronson, *Hype* (New York: William Morrow, 1983), 245.

16. Goodman.

17. Parsons.

18. Diana McLellan, *Ear on Washington* (New York: Arbor House, 1982).

19. "Entertainment Tonight," May 9–12, 1983.

20. Klurfeld, 57.

21. "Entertainment Tonight," May 9–12, 1983.

22. Ibid.

23. Ibid.

24. Ibid.

25. Ibid.

26. Ibid.

27. Ibid.

28. Ibid.

29. Ibid.

30. Ibid.

31. Ibid.

32. Ibid.

33. Ibid.

34. Richard A. Shweder, *New York Times Book Review* (September 21, 1986): 1.


CHAPTER 4

1. James West, *Plainville, U.S.A.* (New York: Columbia University Press, 1945), 162.
2. Sally Engle Merry, "Rethinking Gossip and Scandal." In *Toward a General Theory of Social Control*, ed. by Donald Black (Orlando, FL: Academic Press, 1984).
3. Lewis H. Lapham, Liz Smith, Barbara Howar, William F. Buckley, Jr., John Gross, Mark Crispin Miller, and Robert Darnton, "Gossiping about Gossip," *Harper's* 272 (1986): 40.
4. "Small Percentage of Doctors Responsible for Increase in Suits," *Boston Sunday Globe* (June 15, 1986): 1.
5. Lapham *et al.*, 42.
6. Sally Engle Merry, "Racial Integration in an Urban Neighborhood: The Social Organization of Strangers," *Human Organization* 39 (1980): 59–60.
7. Merry, "Rethinking Gossip and Scandal," 289.
8. Ibid., 292.
9. Lapham *et al.*, 40.
10. Jack Anderson, as quoted in "The Kennedy Debacle," *Newsweek* (August 25, 1969): 75.
11. "People of Massachusetts Rush to Support Kennedy," *New York Times* (July 25, 1969): 10.
12. "How Kennedy Rates with Voters," *U.S. News and World Report* (September 1, 1969): 12.
13. "Public Reaction: Charitable, Skeptical," *Time* (August 1, 1969): 17.
14. Ibid., 14.
15. "Mr. Kennedy's Response," *New York Times* (August 1, 1969): 1.
16. "The Mysteries of Chappaquiddick," *Time* (August 1, 1969): 13.
17. "The Kennedy Debacle," *Newsweek* (August 25, 1969): 75.

18. Warren Weaver, "McGovern Considers '72 Race; Convinced Kennedy Won't Run," *New York Times* (August 13, 1969): 25.
19. Robert McFadden, "Kennedy Kopechne Report Questioned," *New York Times* (February 22, 1976): 1.
20. Steven Roberts, "Many Dreams Are Dying in Boston as Kennedys' Legend Is Tarnished," *New York Times* (February 29, 1976): 26.
21. "The Tide in Ted's Life," *Time* (January 28, 1980): 29.
22. "The Story of Chappaquiddick Back in the News Again," *U.S. News and World Report* (January 28, 1980): 54.
23. "The Tide in Ted's Life," *Time* (January 28, 1980): 28.
24. Dick Hafer, *Every Family Has One* (Washington, DC: Books Inc., 1982).
25. "A Fraud in the Pulitzers," *Time* (April 27, 1981): 52–53.
26. John Walcott and Gerald F. Seib, *Wall Street Journal* (August 25, 1986): 1.
27. "A Bodyguard of Lies," *Newsweek* (October 13, 1986): 46.
28. Our sample consisted of the eighty-one front-page stories appearing in the first Sunday edition of each month.
29. Tyler Abell, *Drew Pearson Diaries 1949–1959* (New York: Holt, Rinehart & Winston, 1974), 359.
30. *Newsweek* (August 25, 1969): 75.
31. Oliver Pilat, *Drew Pearson* (New York: Pocket Books, 1973), 22.
32. Jay R. Nash, *Citizen Hoover* (Chicago: Nelson-Hall, 1972), 199.
33. Ibid.
34. Ibid.
35. Ibid.
36. William Greider, "Trial by Silhouette," *Rolling Stone* (February 17, 1983): 7.
37. "Sexual Congress," *The New Republic* (August 8, 1983): 5.
38. Ibid.
39. "Housecleaning," *Time* (July 25, 1983): 21.
40. Jonathan Alter, "Sex and Pages on Capitol Hill," *Newsweek* (July 25, 1983): 17.
41. "Congress Beset by New Sex Scandal," *U.S. News and World Report* (July 25, 1983): 9.

42. Alter.
43. "Studds Comes Out," *The Nation* (August 20–27, 1983): 132.
44. "Foe of Studds Says Issue is Child Molestation," *New York Times* (June 27, 1984): 22.
45. Robert Bauman, *The Gentlemen from Maryland—The Conscience of a Gay Conservative* (New York: Arbor House, 1986), 12.
46. Ibid., 18.
47. Ibid., 19.
48. Ibid.
49. Ibid., 20.
50. Ibid., 26.
51. Ibid.
52. Ibid., 21.
53. Ibid., 20–21.
54. Ibid., 195.
55. Ibid., 55.
56. Ibid., 71–72.
57. Ibid., 76.
58. Ibid., 141.

## CHAPTER 5

1. Oliver Pilat, *Drew Pearson: An Unauthorized Biography* (New York: Harper's, 1973), 21.
2. Ibid.
3. Ibid., 23.
4. Robert Lindsey, "Carol Burnett and Enquirer Clash in Court," *New York Times* (March 18, 1981): 4.
5. Albin Krebs and Robert Thomas, Jr., "$10 Million Libel Suit against Enquirer Nears Trial," *New York Times* (March 9, 1981): 2.
6. "Trial Opens in Carol Burnett's Libel Suit," *New York Times* (March 12, 1981): 2.
7. "Jury Gives Award of $1.6 Million to Carol Burnett," *Wall Street Journal* (March 27, 1981): 31.
8. "On the Right," *National Review* (May 1, 1983): 509.

9. "Enquirer Belted," *Time* (April 6, 1981): 77.
10. Robert Lindsey, "Carol Burnett Given $1.6 Million in Suit against National Enquirer," *New York Times* (March 27, 1981): A1.
11. "Carol Burnett's Libel Award Cut in Half to $800,000," *New York Times* (May 13, 1981): 3; "Enquirer Belted," *Time* (April 6, 1981): 77.
12. Ibid., 3.
13. "Enquirer Belted," *Time* (April 6, 1981): 77.
14. Rodney A. Smolla, *Suing the Press* (New York: Oxford University Press).
15. Ibid., 6.
16. Ibid.
17. "A Five Year Legal Toothache," *Time* (March 25, 1981): 9.
18. "Currents," *U.S. News and World Report* (April 6, 1981).
19. Smolla, 121.
20. "The Bishop Speaks Out to Silence the Rumors," *Providence Journal-Bulletin* (April 5, 1986): 1.
21. Fredrick Koenig, *Rumor in the Marketplace: The Social Psychology of Commercial Hearsay* (Dover, MA: Auburn House, 1985).
22. We have examined cases of well-known individuals and groups that have been targets of gossip. Given their resources and power, these victims have attempted to combat gossip by going directly to the public in every way possible, including the use of television and the press. Obviously, ordinary people who are victimized by gossip cannot employ these resources, but they might learn something from those who can. Certain gossip-fighting techniques are available to ordinary people.

    Suppose a prying neighbor decides to spoil an individual's reputation by passing malicious lies about his sex life. He is totally innocent, but who's going to believe it? What can he do? First of all, he can take a tip from Bishop Gelineau and Entenmann's Bakery and speak out on his own behalf: silence implies guilt. On the other hand, if he runs from friend to friend with an unproven denial, he risks spreading the lies even further. Instead, he might employ the services of a local version of Walter Cronkite—a credible "public relations person" who is well respected by mutual acquaintances and is willing to approach them with the truth about the victim of gossip. In this way, anyone who continues to spread the nasty version of the tale risks offending the victim's ally, too.

There are, of course, certain situations in which nasty gossip is accurate. When such truthful gossip concerns a violation of a major norm, the responses available to a target are available but are not easy to pursue. Unlike celebrities, who may not be able to hide from mass media exposure, an ordinary person can change jobs, move from a neighborhood or town, or make new friends.

As we have seen, much of everyday gossip is trivial. When truthful gossip concerns a minor blunder or transgression, the victim's reputation may not be harmed at all and may even be strengthened. Celebrity gossip certainly has this characteristic: a little "dirt" in the life story of a Hollywood star only makes the reader more sympathetic. Similarly, gossip about a mistake or transgression on the part of an ordinary individual can even make his or her friends like him or her more. They may see this person as just a little more human and therefore as more worthy of compassion and understanding.

Perhaps the most important lesson to be learned from examining the way that celebrities respond to gossip comes from noting the active role that they play in its transmission. Many Hollywood stars plant their own stories.

Ordinary people can also plant their own gossip. Say that an individual knows someone is about to reveal damaging information about her life. She could sit back and let gossip ruin her reputation, or she could beat them to the punch by circulating her side of the story first. For example, a woman who is going through a nasty divorce might take the initiative away from her estranged husband by quickly planting her side of the story around the neighborhood. She can't stop people from talking, but she can at least exercise some control over what others will say behind her back.

Employers are quick to "leak" gossip that might otherwise hurt them. Before layoffs are announced, the boss has already planted the story on the office grapevine. In no time, the unhappy news has circulated so that every employee knows. The boss has let gossip do the dirty work for him or her!

# SELECTED
# BIBLIOGRAPHY

## PROFESSIONAL SOURCES

Berne, Patricia H., and Louis M. Savary. 1982. *What Will the Neighbors Say?* New York: Continuum.

Bok, Sissela. 1983. *Secrets*. New York: Vintage Books.

Brunvand, Jan Harold. 1981. *The Vanishing Hitchhiker*. New York: W. W. Norton.

Cantor, Muriel, and Susanne Pingree. 1983. *The Soap Opera*. Beverly Hills, CA: Sage.

Cox, B. "What is Hopi Gossip About? Information Management and Hopi Factions." *Man* 5:88–98.

Fine, Gary A.. 1977. "Social Components of Children's Gossip." *Journal of Communication* 27:181–185.

Fine, Gary A. 1983. "Rumors and Gossiping." *Handbook of Discourse Analysis*. London: Academic Press.

Fine, Gary A., and Ralph L. Rosnow. 1978. "Gossip, Gossipers, Gossiping." *Personality and Social Psychology Bulletin* 4:161–168.

Gluckman, Max. 1963. "Gossip and Scandal." *Current Anthropology* 4:307–316.

Haviland, John B. 1977. "Gossip as Competition in Zinacantan." *Journal of Communication* 27:186–191.

Haviland, John B. 1977. *Gossip, Reputation, and Knowledge in Zincantan*. Chicago: Chicago University Press.

Heilman, Samuel C. 1976. *Synagogue Life*. Chicago: University of Chicago.

Jaeger, M. E., S. Anthony, and R. L. Rosnow. 1980. "Who Hears What From Whom and With What Effect: A Study of Rumor." *Personality and Social Psychology Bulletin* 6:473–478.

Koenig, Fredrick. 1985. *Rumor in the Marketplace: The Social Psychology of Commercial Hearsay*. Dover, MA: Auburn House.

Levin, Jack, and Arnold Arluke. 1985. "An Exploratory Analysis of Sex Differences in Gossip." *Sex Roles* 12:281–286.

Levin, Jack, and Allan J. Kimmel. 1977. "Gossip Columns: Media Small Talk." *Journal of Communication* 27:169–175.

Levin, Jack, Amita Mody-Desbareau, and Arnold Arluke. 1986. *The Gossip Tabloid as an Agent of Social Control*. A paper presented at the annual meetings of American Sociological Association, New York.

Medini, G., and E. H. Rosenberg. 1976. "Gossip and Psychotherapy." *American Journal of Psychotherapy* 30:452–462.

Merry, Sally Engle. 1984. "Rethinking Gossip and Scandal." In *Toward a General Theory of Social Control*, ed. by Donald Black. Orlando, FL: Academic Press.

Morin, Edgar. 1971. *Rumour in Orléans*. New York: Random House.

Rosnow, Ralph L. 1977. "Gossip and Marketplace Psychology." *Journal of Communication* 27:158–163.

Rosnow, Ralph L., and Gary A. Fine. 1976. *Rumor and Gossip: The Social Psychology of Hearsay*. New York: Elsevier.

Rosnow, Ralph L., and Marianthi Georgoudi. 1985. "Killed by Idle Gossip: The Psychology of Small Talk." In *When*

*Information Counts,* ed. by Bernard Rubin. Lexington, MA: D. C. Health.

Rysman, Alexander. 1977. "How the 'Gossip' Became a Woman." *Journal of Communication* 27:176–180.

Sabini, John, and Maury Silver. 1982. *Moralities of Everyday Life.* Oxford and New York: Oxford University Press.

Shibutani, Tamotsu. 1966. *Improvised News.* Indianapolis: Bobbs-Merrill.

Shweder, Richard A. 1986. "Storytelling Among the Anthropologists." *New York Times Book Review* (September 21, 1986):1, 38.

Smolla, Rodney A. 1986. *Suing the Press.* New York: Oxford University Press.

Spacks, Patricia Meyers. 1985. *Gossip.* New York: Alfred A. Knopf.

Stirling, R. B. 1956. "Some Psychological Mechanisms Operative in Gossip." *Social Forces* 34:262–267.

Suls, Jerry M. 1977. "Gossip as Social Comparison." *Journal of Communication* 27:164–168.

Yerkovich, Sally. 1977. "Gossiping as a Way of Speaking." *Journal of Communication* 27 (Winter):192–196.

Ziegler, Philip. 1986. "The Lure of Gossip, the Rules of History." *New York Times Book Review* (February 23):1, 34.

## POPULAR SOURCES

Abell, Tyler. 1974. *Drew Pearson: Diaries 1949–1959.* New York: Holt, Rinehart & Winston.

Allen, Steve. 1981. *Funny People.* Briarcliff Manor, NY: Stein & Day.

Aronson, M. L. Steven. 1983. *Hype.* New York: William Morrow.

Barrett, Rona. 1975. *Miss Rona.* New York: Bantam.

Dunn, Angela Fox. 1985. "Gossip Makes the World Go Round." *The Windsor Star* (August 24):C7.

Eells, G. 1972. *Hedda and Louella.* New York: Warner.

Goodman, Ezra. 1962. *The Fifty Year Decline and Fall of Hollywood.* New York: Macfadden.

Graham, Sheilah. 1969. *Confessions of a Hollywood Columnist*. New York: William Morrow.

Higham, Charles. 1979. *Celebrity Circus*. New York: Delacorte Press.

Howar, Barbara. 1973. *Laughing All the Way*. New York: Stein & Day.

Klurfeld, Herman. 1976. *Winchell, His Life and Times*. New York: Praeger.

Lapham, Lewis H., Liz Smith, Barbara Howar, William F. Buckley, Jr., John Gross, Mark Crispin Miller, and Robert Darnton. 1986. "Gossiping about Gossip." *Harper's* 272:37–50.

Lowman, Josephine. 1983. "Some Gossip Actually Could Be Good for You." *Champagne-Urbana News Gazette* (June):4.

Malatesta, Kathleen. 1980. "The Inside Story of the Supermarket Sensationals." *Comment* (Spring):12–15.

McLellan, Diana. 1982. *Ear on Washington*. New York: Arbor House.

Niven, David. 1975. *Bring on the Empty Horses*. New York: Dell.

Nolan, Martin F. 1986. "Gossip's Sorry State." *Boston Globe* (April 17):A1, A20.

Parsons, Louella O. 1961. *Tell It To Louella*. New York: Putnam.

Peterson, Norma. 1986. "Putting Loose Lips to Good Use." *USA Today* (April 9):4D.

Pilat, Oliver. 1973. *Drew Pearson: An Unauthorized Biography*. New York: Harper's.

Thomas, Bob. 1971. *Winchell*. Garden City, NY: Doubleday.

"Tidbits of Gossip Nibble at Press." 1983. *USA Today* (May 16):10A.

Young, Julie. 1986. "Sensational Stories are Adult 'Fairy Tales.' " *The Daily Progress* (June 19):D1.

# INDEX